Skiing Legends

and

The Laurentian Lodge Club

Neil and Catharine McKenty

Durham, NC

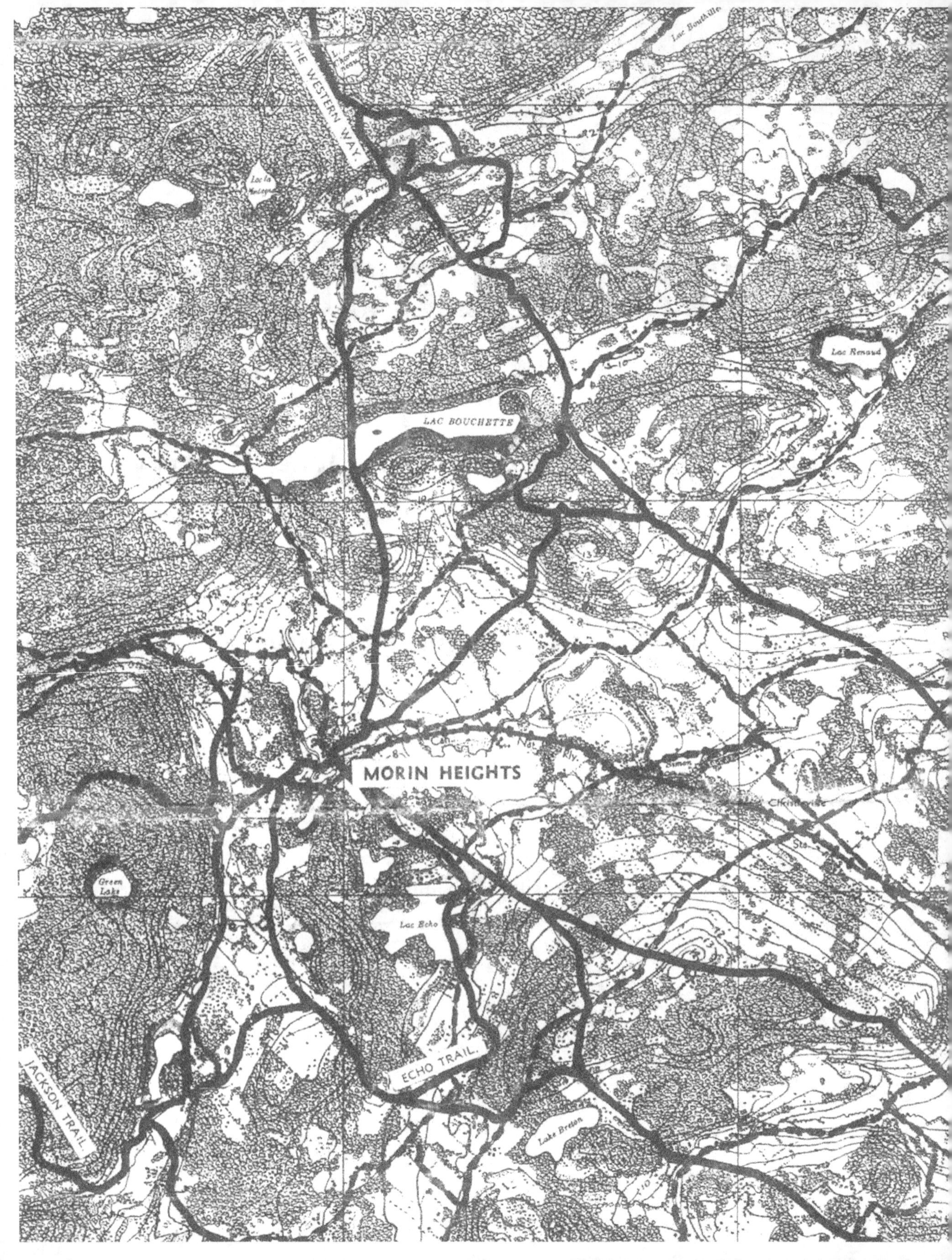
THE WESTERN WAY
LAC BOUCHETTE
Lac Renaud
MORIN HEIGHTS
Green Lake
Lac Echo
ECHO TRAIL
JACKSON TRAIL
Lake Breton

OLD WOC TRAIL
STE. ADELE
WOC TRAIL
WOC HOUSE
MONT ROLLAND
Range
TRAIL
ST. MARGARET TRAIL
BARN HILL
BEER SIGN HILL
MARIBOU TRAIL
PIEDMONT
EUR DES MONTS
RED BIRDS' HOUSE
RED BIRDS' DOWNHILL RUN
FOSTER'S RUN
LONE ELM
DOUGLAS TRAIL
LUMBER TRAIL
SHAWBRIDGE
BIG HILL
WEST TRAIL
Lac Violon
Lac Ste. Adèle
Lac Marois
Lac Millet
Lac Guindon

Skiing Legends
and The Laurentian Lodge Club
Neil and Catharine McKenty
http://neilmckenty.com

Third edition 2013
Published 2001 by Price-Patterson Ltd.
Canadian Publishers, Montreal, Quebec

Published 2019, by Light Messages Publishing
www.lightmessages.com
Durham, NC 27713 USA
SAN: 920-9298

Paperback ISBN: 978-1-61153-083-4
Hardcover ISBN: 978-1-61153-755-0
E-book ISBN: 978-1-61153-447-4
Library of Congress Control Number: 2019945720

Front and back covers designed by Studio Melrose/Ted Sancton
using CPR archive photos

For all the members,
past, present, and future,
of the Laurentian Lodge Club
and all those who love skiing
the world over.

AUTHOR'S PREFACE

Be careful what you pray for because you can't be sure what you'll get. And be careful when you write a book because you never know where it'll take you.

Skiing Legends and the Laurentian Lodge Club started as a story about a ski club in the village of Shawbridge (now Prévost) which began in 1923 and may well be the oldest residential ski club in North America. But quickly this story, like a pair of runaway skis, developed a momentum of its own leading willy-nilly to discovering the Club's place in the history of the Laurentians and the men and women who skied them. Quickly the names came tumbling forth, like the skiers at the end of a "bushwhacking race" – "Jackrabbit" Johannsen, Percy Douglas, Harry Pangman, the Cochands and the skiing sisters, the Kemps, the Wurteles and the Parés, the Montreal Ski Club, the McGill Red Birds and the Penguins.

And there are still more storied names – Viscount d'Ivry, "the remittance man", the Duke de Leuchtenberg, Augustin Morin and Curé Labelle, Harry Wheeler, Joe Ryan, General Panet and Earl Alexander of Tunis. So many names. So many stories.

This is the story of those names and many more, the story of a time when Montrealers skied on Mount Royal on barrel staves, when Lumkin's Hotel on Côte-des-Neiges was the place tired skiers relaxed with a hot toddy before the fire, when the Laurentian ski trains, shrouded in steam and frost, were festive with the tinkle of ukeleles, sing-songs and the warm glow from the over-hanging gas lamps.

This is the story of the Ryans, Joe and Mary, welcoming their guests at Mont-Tremblant, and the Wheelers, George and Alice, stoking the fireplace at Gray Rocks and Mrs. Marshall serving baked beans, brown bread and black coffee at her boarding house to the skiers getting off at Shawbridge, the "gateway to the Laurentians". The Laurentian Lodge Club (more familiarly called the Shawbridge Club) has, for seventy-seven years, been at the heart of Shawbridge, reflecting Montrealers at their favourite winter playground.

So many members over the years – business people, lawyers, doctors, teachers, senators, journalists, cabinet ministers, nurses, parents, children. So many names. So many stories.

It's not surprising that about three years ago, several members of the Shawbridge Club thought these names, these stories, this history of the Laurentians were worth preserving. They approached my wife, Catharine, and she began collecting material from current and past Club members, helped immeasurably in this painstaking task by the enthusiastic support of another club member, Sally Drummond.

I only became seriously involved about a year ago after Catharine and Sally had amassed a treasure-trove of material, mostly personal recollections and after Catharine had scoured the whole country for photographs. When I realized this material was so rich historically (the challenge was not which reminiscences to put in but which, sadly, to leave out), I decided to get on board.

I cannot mention all who helped but my wife was with me every step of the way, providing fresh material, suggesting editorial changes, restoring my ruffled feathers. Cynthia Macdonald cheerfully provided secretarial help. For advice about the early material on the pre-history of the Laurentians, I am grateful to Professor Toby Morantz of the Department of Anthropology at McGill University and to Venitia Bodycomb, a doctoral candidate at McGill in the Department of Earth and Planetary Sciences.

My editor, Michael Ballantyne, made the book read better and my publisher, Michael Price, made it look better.

The result of all our efforts is *Skiing Legends and The Laurentian Lodge Club*. We hope the story reflects, in a fresh way, a slice of life in Montreal and in the Laurentians that it would be a pity to leave unchronicled. We had fun doing it. We hope you have fun reading about it.

Neil McKenty

Westmount, September 8, 2000

CONTENTS

PRELUDE

It was New Year's Eve, 1952, at the Laurentian Lodge Club in the foothills of the Laurentian mountains. The members, out of their snowy ski togs and dressed to the nines, were sipping their pre-dinner drinks in the comfortable lounge, beside the Christmas tree and the blazing fieldstone fireplace. There was an air of anticipation. Word had gone round that a special announcement, somehow related to the Club, was presently to be made by Buckingham Palace.

Dr. Wilder Penfield, founder of the Montreal Neurological Institute, joined the Shawbridge Club in 1930.

(Penfield Archives, Osler Library, McGill University)

A young man, sporting a McGill blazer, walked over to the floor-model Marconi radio and turned the dials, so high the little children of Club members had to stretch to reach them. There was a crackle of static before the news came on. The members crowded close to hear. One of them was smoking his pipe, a tall man in a grey herringbone suit over a red vest, a Princeton pin in his lapel.

Then the announcer read the item from Buckingham Palace with the prominent names on the Queen's Honours List for the New Year, 1953. Her Majesty, Queen Elizabeth the Second, had bestowed the Order of Merit, the highest civilian decoration in the British Empire, on Montreal's renowned neurosurgeon, Wilder Penfield.

There were cheers, toasts and congratulations all round. Only one Canadian, the country's longest serving Prime Minister, the Right Honourable Mackenzie King, had ever received the O.M., which could be held by no more than twenty-four people at a single time.

Dr. Penfield and his family had been members of the Shawbridge Club since 1930. Now he was sixty-one, a trim balding man with the square shoulders of the athlete he had been at Princeton University, just over six feet tall, with an expression and smile that resembled President Eisenhower's. He was an imposing but not intimidating figure, at least not at the Club where he was sometimes referred to as "the gentle giant".

A keen skier himself, Dr. Penfield was often among the first to hear the early morning call, "Who's for skiing this morning? Get a move on. All out." It was a man's voice, "clear and high," he remembered, "like the voice of a yodeler at the start of his yodel." The voice belonged to the most famous skier of them all, Herman "Jackrabbit" Smith Johannsen, who had been a member of the Shawbridge Club almost since its beginning in 1923.

Many a morning, the "Jackrabbit" skied over to the Club from his little house nearby, rousted up a group, clomped to the front door in sight of the Big Hill, snapped on his skis and, at the head of his chattering retinue, thin and craggy as a pine tree, swooshed through the powdery snow towards the heart of the mountains.

"This strong, wiry man with the profile of an eagle, Johannsen, is the Pied Piper, one might say, of the ski hills. He called in his clear, high voice and the young and the strong came flocking after him to discover the cold, white beauty of the North." **Wilder Penfield** (CPR collection)

MANITOU EWITCHI

More than a billion years ago, a lumbering land mass collided with the Precambrian Shield, squeezing the oceans between. In this collision, rocks buckled and scrunched up like sheets of plasticine crushed at both ends. Out of this upheaval emerged the mountains we now call the Laurentians, probably as high then as the Rockies are today.

Meanwhile, deep in the belly of the earth, red hot rocks flowed upward under the surface of the continents, splitting them apart and, from this fiery maelstrom, forming a basin for the ancient Iapetus Ocean. About six hundred million years ago, the waters along its western coast encroached on the subsiding land and the Laurentians stood on the shore of this warm, shallow sea, basking in the tropical temperature. In these same waters, sediment accumulated that later formed the rock on which Montreal now stands.

After more cycles of collisions and upheavals, about a million years ago, tons of glacial ice formed and flattened the Laurentians. These ponderously moving glaciers, like great icy balls of steel wool, scraped and gouged the mountains, polishing them down to the bedrock.

Some 100,000 years ago, these ice caps coalesced to form the Laurentian Ice Sheet, a sea of ice four times as high as Mont-Tremblant. The pressure of this ice weighed on the mountains, smoothing and rounding them into softer bosomy shapes. Finally, some 12,000 years ago, this sea of ice began to melt and recede. Slowly out of the steaming mists, the Laurentians emerged, crowned by the majestic Tremblant, much as we see them today.

Glacial Rock near Ste-Agathe-des-Monts.
(Photo Côté Collection, Ste-Agathe)

As the ice sheets retreated, the climate, warmer than ours is, was able to sustain vegetation, forests of birch and aspen groves, deer, caribou and small game. Then after the ages of granite and ice came the first humans to gaze on the rolling purple hills from the top of Tremblant which they called "Manitou Ewitchi", the mountain of the mysterious Manitou, the spirit in all things.

These first peoples of the Laurentians came by a roundabout route. About 12,000 years ago, the ice sheets subsiding, hunters began to follow animals crossing the Beringian Plain joining Siberia and Alaska. Some of these groups penetrated lands, now the western United States, where they hunted the bison and caribou that grazed the grasslands up to the icy edges of the tundra.

Manitou Ewitchi (Photo Jan Brunner)

Some moved northward, probably using snowshoes, and eventually roving bands of hunters reached the Laurentian region about 6,000 years ago. Among these would have been the ancestors of the Algonquian-speaking peoples who gazed at Tremblant about 1,500 years ago, when Justinian the Emperor was leading the Byzantine Empire and Augustine of Canterbury was beginning his evangelization of Britain.

From the outset, the Algonquins had a religious connection with Tremblant, “Manitou Ewitchi”, the dreaded spirit. Often, they called on their most important figure, the shaman, to ward off evil spirits and to placate the mountain. Their “vision quest” associated them with a preternatural “guardian helper”, who showed them how to live in harmony with nature.

Those who disobeyed nature’s laws risked the wrath of “Manitou Ewitchi”; those who obeyed them would smell the flowers, drink clear water, enjoy pure air and revel in the songs of many birds. The sacred laws of nature prescribed by the Council of the Manitou were three: do not kill except to defend yourself or by necessity; love even the most humble plant; respect the trees.

And so for many a moon in the Laurentians, still unknown to any white man, the first native peoples tried to live in peace and harmony with nature. In summer in birch bark canoes they themselves had invented, in winter on their sleds, toboggans and snowshoes and, in all seasons, they revered “Manitou Ewitchi”

LE ROI DU NORD

After Champlain and the first Europeans appeared in the New World some 400 years ago, the Algonquins became embroiled in the fur trade and in the bitter British-French-Indian wars of the seventeenth century.

In 1653, the Iroquois drove the hunters of the "Petite Nation" into a corner on the shores of le Petit-Lac-Nominingue where they, with their families, were massacred. A little more than a hundred years later, loyalist refugees and soldiers fleeing the American Revolution in 1776 fetched up in the lower Laurentians where they began farming. Scottish settlers joined them when the federal government urged Britain to encourage emigration to Canada. In the 1840s, a large number of Swiss Protestants emigrated to the area, a development the Catholic Church in Quebec viewed with alarm.

Early settlers in Ste-Agathe area (Photo Côté Collection)

As a result, the Church called on French Canadians to settle in the Laurentians north of St-Jérôme (incorporated in 1834) so that as many Catholic parishes as possible could be established. So in the 1840s many Catholics, answering the summons of their church and of their elites, settled between St-Jérôme and Ste-Agathe to try their hand at farming. A decade later, they were joined by a wave of Irish and other immigrants.

Laurentian sawmill (CNR Collection)

From the outset, farming was back-breaking work. One historian of the period describes farming in "the back country" around Morin Heights:

"Frequently a settler cleared only ten or fifteen acres after as many years on the land; on this small clearing whether Irishman or French-Canadian, he grew an acre or two of wheat – growing season permitting – two or three acres of oats, perhaps one acre of potatoes and peas and another of barley and rye. Almost always he had one cow and two or three pigs and often a horse and a small flock of sheep."

To give the hard-pressed farmers a hand was the aim of one of the early Laurentian legends. Augustin-Norbert Morin was a founder of Laval University, a leading politician and the man who launched the famous newspaper, *La Minerve.* He established the first parish in Ste-Adèle, and many places in the Laurentians, such as Val-Morin and Lac-Morin (later Lake Manitou) were named for him.

Curé Labelle, "Le Roi du Nord", 1889
(Collection La Société d'histoire de la Rivière-du-Nord.)

In 1852, while in the government of Lower Canada and in order to stimulate agriculture in the north, Morin set up an experimental potato farm in Ste-Adèle. The experiment fizzled because the soil in the region, devastated by the moving glaciers, was too thin and anemic to sustain much in the way of crops and cattle. So during the next decade the homesteaders turned from the farm to the forest. At this time Britain, with a vast empire to protect, was devouring wood the way a lion devours lesser breeds, a welcome development for Laurentian farmers who increasingly looked to the pine tree for a livelihood.

In the 1850s, the demand for wood from the saw mills outstripped the need for squared logs so communities like Shawbridge (incorporated in 1840) began to grow as the mills strung along the Rivière-du-Nord (the waterway spine of the Laurentians) shipped their output downstream to the Ottawa river and on to Hawkesbury where the Hamilton company was among the largest producers of cut lumber in North America. Still, even by the mid-Sixties, when logging and lumbering reached their peak, the population between St-Jérôme and Ste-Agathe was as thin as the soil. Fortunately, one of the greatest of all the Laurentian legends was about to change that.

Curé François-Xavier Antoine Labelle was born in 1833 in Ste-Rose, the son of a shoemaker. He was ordained a priest for the Roman Catholic Archdiocese of Montreal in 1856 and two years later was appointed to a wealthy parish in St-Jérôme. The appointment was no accident. For some time, Curé Labelle had been concerned about the loss of French Catholic homesteaders in the north to the mills and factories of the New England states and he often spoke of his concern with his superior, Bishop Ignace Bourget.

When he arrived at his new parish, Curé Labelle, more than six feet tall and tipping the scales at 300 pounds, was an energetic imposing figure, an ingratiating mixture of authority and charm. His parishioners and others regarded him with awe. From his first days in St-Jérôme, Curé Labelle proclaimed his dream of developing a chain of parishes from St-Jérôme through the mountains and the valleys along the Rivière-du-Nord past the Ontario border and beyond the Red River valley in Manitoba. He would people these parishes in this thousand-mile corridor with French-speaking Catholics.

And the Curé had a second dream. He went on many a hunting and fishing trip with his friends to the Valley of the Devil's River, north of Ste-Agathe. So rugged was the terrain that they called it "La Repousse". But Curé Labelle saw beyond the hardships to the spec-tacular beauty of the Laurentians and their potential as a recreation region: "Cars full of tourists will be seen arriving here," he wrote after one of his many trips to Tremblant. Sometimes, he would stand beside his tent in the evening, gazing at the soft mysterious shape of the mountains themselves, at the dark vastness of the forests and the purple pools of light enveloping the meadows and colouring the distant lakes like a priestly stole.

One of Curé Labelle's thirty expeditions into the Laurentians

His great friend, William Henry Scott, whose family were the original owners of the Laurentian Lodge property, accompanied him at least twice, and wrote an account of their four-day trek in October, 1869, to reach the Rivière du Diable, later the site of St-Jovite. (Archives du Diocèse de St-Jérôme)

But Curé Labelle knew that if his people were to come to this magnificent playground, they would need transport. In 1868, the train from Montreal did not go even as far as St-Jérôme. An attempt to resurface the "corduroy" road to St-Jérôme was opposed by Montreal's politicians on the grounds it would cost too much.

However, the exceptionally severe winter of 1871-72 provided the Curé with the leverage he needed. There was a shortage of firewood in Montreal which led to much hardship and illness. Curé Labelle seized on this to demonstrate to Montrealers how much they would benefit from easy access to the Laurentians. He organized a bee to collect firewood and a jingling caravan of eighty sleighs took it to hundreds of Montreal families who desperately needed this fuel for cooking and heating. Curé Labelle had a natural flair for good public relations. He organized a second "wood train", this time with a hundred sleighs led by a brass band and a team of six magnificent horses caparisoned with red pompoms pulling the vehicle, draped with a large tricolour flag, from which the Curé and M. Villemure, the mayor of St-Jérôme, waved to the applauding crowds on Montreal's streets. In the next few years, through their taxes, grateful Montrealers contributed more than a million dollars to the first stage of the Curé's dream, extending the railroad to St-Jérôme.

The first train to St-Jérôme left Montreal Sept. 16, 1876 On October 9, Curé Labelle celebrated with 200 of his friends in the enormous mill hall in St-Jérôme.

(Collection La Société d'histoire de la Rivière-du-Nord)

Not to be outdone, the man who charmed politicians both in Ottawa and Quebec City and was now called "Le Roi du Nord", was able to get a National Lottery approved so as to further his dreams for the Laurentians. One of only four lotteries authorized in the province in the nineteenth century, the tickets cost a dollar apiece for a grand prize of $10,000, an immense sum in those days.

So in 1876, wreathed in a cloud of whistling steam, the first engine pulling "le P'tit Train du Nord" rumbled into the St-Jérôme station to cheers that echoed through the hills. Curé Labelle's dream of the Laurentians as a tourist playground was coming true. Actually, as early as the 1870s, some wealthy Montrealers, travelling by horse and buggy on roads that were not much more than wagon tracks, were buying recreational properties around Lake Manitou, a few miles north of Ste-Agathe. One of the first was Philip Durnford, member of a distinguished British military family.

As a boy, Philip Durnford had lived in the province while his father was directing the construction of the Citadel in Quebec City. Philip returned to Canada in 1835 and ten years later settled in Montreal where he was appointed the federal Collector of Inland Revenue. He often explored the Laurentians as far north as Lac-Cornu near Nantel, a two-day journey by horse and buggy with a stopover in St-Jérôme. In 1871, he bought a block of lots just north of Lake Manitou for which he paid the princely sum of $155.10. This estate, eventually numbering some 2,000 acres, stayed in the Durnford family for a hundred years and is now the Valdurn development. Philip Durnford (one of whose descendants, former Gazette writer Nancy Durnford Lorimer, is a member of the Shawbridge Club), thus became one of the first owners of a holiday property in the Laurentians.

By the 1880s, the area between Shawbridge and Ste-Agathe and beyond was attracting miners, loggers, wranglers, lumberjacks, hunters and vacationers. Throw in some hard drinkers, a few loose women and frequent fist fights, it was little wonder this incendiary mix led staid Montrealers to view the upper Laurentians as "the wild west of the French world". The coming of the railroads in the Nineties changed the mix for good because it also marked the beginning of the fulfillment of Curé Labelle's dream of the Laurentians as one of this country's premier recreation regions.

Early Snow Train (Photo Côté Collection)

In 1888, one of the Curé's fishing companions, Honoré Mercier, the premier of Quebec, appointed him deputy minister in the new Department of Agriculture and Colonization, probably the first time in North America that a priest had held so important a public office. In 1890, the train came to Shawbridge, to Ste-Adèle the next year and on a warm September day in 1892, to Ste-Agathe where a large group of politicians and other dignitaries, suitably solemn in their shiny black frock coats, top hats and walrus moustaches, stood by the tracks to cheer it on.

Sadly, there was a gaping hole in that august assembly. The man who had been the driving force behind rail and road development and who had done more than anyone to excite people to pitch their tents in his beloved Laurentians was not there to see his dream come true. Curé Labelle, the father of colonization, "le Roi de Nord", had died the year before, aged fifty-eight, following a hernia operation. Today the highway named to honour his great achievements (Route 117) is only a short ski from the Shawbridge Club.

MR. BIRCH

Meanwhile, back in Montreal in the mid-Nineties, sleighing, skating and extravaganzas like the sculptured winter ice palaces caught the attention of so prestigious a journal as Harper's Weekly: "Since Russia and Canada cannot be moved ten or twelve degrees toward the tropics ... their people do well not merely to fence themselves against the cold with such palliatives as furs and blubber and hot toddies, but to maintain that they enjoy the winter".

Mr. Birch, 1879

(Barbara Douglas Tindale Collection)

The enjoyment of the winter in the last quarter of the nineteenth century in Montreal did not include much skiing. When *The Gazette* on January 7, 1877, listed amusements for a winter's day including curling and coasting on river ice, skiing was not on the programs.

That situation changed in the first week of February 1879, when a few Montrealers witnessed a curious sight – a tall bearded man, dressed in a full-length overcoat with a brightly coloured sash and a fur hat, apparently sliding forward on a pair of long boards. *The Canadian Illustrated News* reported on this phenomenon in its issue of February 8, 1879:

"Mr. A. Birch, a Norwegian gentleman of Montreal, has a pair of patent Norwegian snowshoes upon which he has taken a trip to Quebec starting Friday last. The snowshoes are entirely of wood, nine feet long, six inches wide and have a footboard and toe strap. He walks with the aid of a pole and crosses ice not buoyant enough to bear a good sized dog, so buoyant are the shoes in action".

So buoyant was Mr. Birch in action that H. Percy Douglas, a pioneer skier and one of the first members of the Shawbridge Club, remarks in his colourful book, *My Skiing Years*, that a trek of 170 miles from Montreal to Quebec City would be a tremendous feat even today using the most modern equipment.

Soon after Mr. Birch led the way, more Montrealers took up skiing. Tom Drummond, also a pioneer skier and one of the founders in 1904 of the Montreal Ski Club, writes that as early as 1880 a few daring members of Montreal's snowshoe clubs discovered in skiing "a new source of thrills and enjoyment". Drummond also spotted a few skiers on Mount Royal about 1881.

Gradually, more Montrealers seeking "thrills and enjoyment" took up skiing so that *The Gazette* on February 10, 1887, could report:

"On Saturday evening a few ubiquitous athletes attacked the Priests' Farm near the Montreal Toboggan slide with ski or 'Norwegian Snowshoe'. The start was from the highest point on the other side of Côte-des-Neiges-Road. Of the party two were greenhorns while the third claimed experience which, however, helped him little. They met all sorts of difficulties and their guiding staffs were of little help. After many adventures they returned home exhibiting their newly acquired skills on Ste-Catherine Street under the full glare of the street lights, to a large and appreciative audience."

A decade later some of the McGill staff were already skiing when, in 1899, a few professors, including Percy Nobbs, a well-known architect who designed the University Club

Huntly Drummond (far left) with friends, 1909, at the N.E. corner of Sherbrooke and McTavish, now site of the McLennan Library

(Bruce McNiven Collection)

and the war memorial in the Town of Mount Royal, got together to ski on Mount Royal during the evening. After supper, the professors would grab their equipment and head for the mountain, their ten-foot Finnish skis turned up at both ends with a loose toe strap and a seal-skin footpad to avoid back-slip. Although Montreal's streets were ploughed, snow removal was non-existent and the banks on either side often rose as high as six or eight feet. The professors would slide down the long silent streets between Pine and Sherbrooke, then kick off their skis and plod up to the top again.

Percy Nobbs writes that night skiing could be hazardous "as it was not uncommon for a ski to come off and go snaking down the hill riderless". One night, it was reported that a dog running loose had been transfixed by a runaway ski. In fact, considering the professors did not use ski poles, which did not come into popular use until just before the First World War, their control hurtling down between the snow banks of Peel street was all the more remarkable.

"The Meeting Place"
Members of the Montreal Ski Club climb towards their first clubhouse at the foot of Côte-des-Neiges hill c. 1920.
(Haagen Kierulf Collection)

At the time the McGill professors were skiing in the evenings on Mount Royal, the city, whose lights they could see winking beneath them, was the cultural and commercial centre of Canada, numbering a population of 140,000 people. As W. D. Lighthall, three times mayor of Westmount – and a renaissance man – wrote in *Montreal after 250 Years,* Montreal possessed an old world charm flavoured with the exciting possibilities of frontier Canada. (At this time Ste-Agathe was considered the frontier to the north.) *The Dominion Illustrated News* of February 9, 1889, waxed lyrical about Montreal's pre-eminence: "Looking down from its Olympian Heights, it surveyed a sporting scene unique in the world and unparalleled in Canadian sporting history".

Nor was it any accident that Mr. Birch, the first reported skier in Montreal, was a Norwegian. Norway was the birthplace of skiing (the first evidence we have for skis goes back 6,000 years) but the sport initially caught the public's imagination in 1888 when Fridtjof Nansen, a young Norwegian with a drive to explore, led a group on skis across the Greenland icecap.

But even before Nansen's remarkable achievement fired the public imagination and enthusiasm for skiing began to grow, particularly in Europe, another Norwegian, who would become the most famous member of the Shawbridge Club, was already trying out his first pair of skis. Born in 1875 in the hamlet of Horten in the forest outside Oslo, Herman Smith Johannsen began skiing at the age of two. Sixty years on, he would give this advice to his young charges at the Shawbridge Club: "You don't need any lessons to ski. It comes naturally. All you need to do is to imitate someone who's doing it a little bit better than you. That's what I did. I watched some older boys."

He learned well, did the boy his fellow Laurentian skiers – or was it his friends the Cree – later dubbed the "Jackrabbit" because he bounced along on his skis as nimbly as a hare. Mr. Johannsen, also called "Chief", would become a legend in his own time, not only for his contribution to skiing in the Laurentians but in many other places around the world.

Just after the turn of the century, the history of skiing in Montreal took a leap forward. The informal nightly arrangements of the skiing professors became more structured when the

Montreal Ski Club, the first organisation of its kind in Canada, was created in 1904. The Club began with the challenging, not to say intimidating, slogan, "Every man, woman, boy or girl in Montreal out on skis or in their graves". Nevertheless, no fewer than fifty members joined the Club immediately and started jumping, first at Fletcher's Field, then on a more suitable hill on Westmount Boulevard near Clarke Avenue. *The Gazette* predicted the Montreal Ski Club would offer its members "the combined pleasures of tobogganing, snowshoeing and skating".

Emily Yates in the Laurentians c. 1920. Early skier on Mount Royal, Red Cross nurse. Visited the Shawbridge Club with Percy Douglas (Henry Yates Collection)

Still, despite this activity, Percy Nobbs, one of McGill's skiing professors and the first president of the Montreal Ski Club, estimates that at the turn of the century Montreal contained no more than a hundred skiers. Few of these were women who, in the early days of the sport, were tolerated rather than encouraged. Among the first women in Montreal to take up the sport were Ruth and Allison Aird, Audrey Thorne and Emily Yates. One afternoon, Percy Douglas watched this group on the mountain. He writes with some astonishment that "they had the audacity to pull kick turns on us and a telemark, something we had been trying to learn all season."

The mountain was the centre of skiing in Montreal and in 1909 the first Canadian Ski Championships were held there. After the competition, Douglas writes "everybody made a dash for Lumkin's famous hotel, 'just around the corner', where the judges figured out the results, and the rest of us sat around comfortably in our private room enjoying a few on the house."

Later when the Montreal Ski Club got a clubhouse of its own on the mountain, the members would repair there after a bracing Sunday morning of skiing. Percy Douglas describes how "we soon come to the clubhouse, all comfortably tired and ravenously hungry:

"The big room is cheery with the six-foot logs burning in the open fireplace, bidding defiance to the ten below temperature outside ... the room is filled with ... merry chatter over the morning's adventures.

Lumkin's Hotel on Queen Mary Road at Côte-des-Neiges, Montreal 1896

(Notman Photographic Archives McCord Museum of Canadian History, Montreal)

"What an appetite! How good a hot cup of strong black tea is after the strenuous workou t! There are beans as only Mrs. Prescott can serve them, and a slab of pie with Canadian cheese. Who could ask for more or better?"

And despite the scarcity of skiers in Montreal, you might catch a glimpse of them on the mountain on Saturday afternoon, (Saturday morning was still not a holiday for most Montrealers), wearing high boots, riding knickers, woollen underwear, sweaters and over all a coloured Mackinaw finished with woollen or fur mitts and a pull-down cap. They had no poles and ski wax was still unknown. A tallow candle was the only remedy for sticky snow but linseed oil and turpentine rubbed into the skis helped their glide. Even with their cumbersome "Norwegian Snowshoes" Montreal's first skiers (some of whom would become members of the Shawbridge Club) learned to stem, to maintain control and, as Percy Douglas put it, "if our dependable telemark failed, we just sat down and hoped for the best."

Most certainly, the members of the Montreal Ski Club did not just sit down and hope for the best. In fact in 1905 its more enterprising members made history. They headed north for the first organized skiing excursion to the central Laurentians, an area of about 600 square miles running north from Shawbridge to Mont-Tremblant, west to Morin Heights and east to a line bisecting Lac-Masson near Ste-Marguerite. Their train, lumbering along from Mile End station to Ste-Agathe, faced its own hazards. The coaches in which they stacked their skis were nothing more than wooden boxes, a stove blazing at one end and passengers' seats down the side. The skiers had to be careful of the boisterous lumberjacks, wranglers and miners squirting streams of yellowish-brown tobacco juice aimed at the silver-plated spittoons along the aisle.

After they disembarked at Ste-Agathe, dressed in their blue breeches and coloured caps pulled down to shield them against the sun, they set off for the nearby Manitou Club which played a role in the founding of the Shawbridge Club almost twenty years later. A group of locals who gathered at the station to watch the train rolling in, its whistle blowing, wreathed in clouds of steam and frost, were astonished to see these skiers gliding through the snow on what resembled smoothed down barrel staves, a mode of transport unknown to them.

After stopping for refreshments at the palatial Manitou Club, Percy Douglas got his first good look at the expanse and beauty of the Laurentians:

"It was overpowering country to me. The great hills, long slopes, fences buried under drifts, trails through the snow-clad woods, across lakes and rivers, tracks of deer, fox and rabbit; all were an entirely new experience. The weather was perfect – fine sunny days and powder snow, and noon-times as hot as a day in midsummer. Lunch was cooked on a height of land in the lee of a great boulder, as we sat drinking in the views of the mountains to the north. The old Manitou was a wonderfully comfortable place and a great rendezvous in those days for snowshoe parties."

Next day – the trip to the Manitou Club would become an annual event and involved staying the weekend – the Montreal skiers stunned the locals when they set off on a trek of thirty miles over the hills to Shawbridge, swinging along without poles.

As expeditions to the Laurentians became more frequent – Shawbridge was usually the jumping-off place or the destination – Mrs. Marshall's famous boarding-house in the village near the bridge across the North River was usually the meeting place. Mrs. Marshall, who would later often have tea with the Hardings at the Shawbridge Club, was famous for her geniality and her table – baked beans, brown bread and strong black coffee. Her boarding-house also exemplified

Visit of Montreal Ski Club to the Manitou Club, 1905

(Notman Photographic Archives, McCord Museum of Canadian History, Montreal)

another advantage of cross-country skiing, the camaraderie and the richness of new friendships, two of the characteristics of the Shawbridge Club later on.

Notwithstanding these annual trips of the Montreal skiers to the Manitou Club, there was little organized skiing in the Laurentians until Émile Cochand from France appeared on the scene in 1911. His son, Louis, remembers the story of his father's entry into Canada:

Skiers coming out of Mrs. Marshall's (left) and the Bridge House (Canadian Ski Museum Collection)

"He was brought over by the manager of the Ritz-Carlton Hotel, a Swiss, who saw my father win the Swiss National Championships in 1909 and said, 'Émile, I'm going to bring you out to teach skiing in Canada.' Émile was a ski instructor with the Swiss Battalion, the ski troops. He came over in 1911 bringing a hundred pairs of Swiss skis with him. The Customs in St. John's didn't know what to make of them; they had only seen snowshoes. He also brought twenty Davos-Luges and six four-man bobsleds."

Émile Cochand then established the region's first ski school at the Laurentide Inn in Ste-Agathe. He opened the Chalet Cochand in 1914, frequented by Montrealers and American skiers (Pierre Trudeau stayed there with his family when he was eleven in 1930). Soon Chalet Cochand became known not only as a place to ski, but also a great place to party and for lady skiers there was the added attraction of Émile's two sons, Louis and Pierre.

Louis Cochand learned to ski at the age of three on barrel staves, gum boots and leather toe-straps. Skilled carpenters would steam the barrel stave or wood-shaped slats and, to keep a curve in the front tip, would attach a double wire from the toe wooden plate to the tip of the ski, then tighten the wire until the tip of the ski bent. They left the staves to dry for twenty-four hours, then released the wires.

It was on these kinds of skis that some members of the Shawbridge Club first learned the sport. At the end of World War One, Gerry Allen learned to ski in Ottawa on barrel staves. Hugh

Seybold, in 1916, strapped on similar skis at the age of six: "At first I used my mother's skis. The whole thing was to find a hill and build a jump. We did this in Westmount Park, and I spent a lot of time in the little gully to the left of the big ski jump near the tennis club."

In 1912 skis, still considered the poor man's snowshoe, received a boost from an unexpected quarter. That year the acclaimed Arctic explorer, Fridtjof Nansen, who had first skied across the Greenland ice cap, was staying with his daughter at the Lake Placid Club in the Adirondacks. To the astonishment of his fellow guests, Nansen, then fifty, climbed Whiteface Mountain on skis, not as some kind of stunt, but as the normal way to do it. Before long, some of the local skiers were cutting cross-country trails as Cochand was doing in the Laurentians.

Ski Instructor Émile Cochand and pupil 1911 (Canadian Ski Museum Collection)

It was in 1912, too, that Montreal became the locale for one of the world's first ski films. A crew from Russia showed up to shoot the winter scenes for a film whose romantic climax featured two young eloping love birds skiing down a mountain pursued by the villain brandishing a Russian sword almost as long as his skis. Half-way down, the villain takes a fearful tumble and the two lovers, saved in the nick of time, ski off into the woods below.

Montrealers, who saw the finished product, cheered at all the appropriate places but they were even more intrigued watching some of the scenes being filmed: Russian signs plastered on the outside of the Ritz-Carlton; strangers in colourful costumes strolling the streets; and Droshky sleighs, pulled by three foam-flecked horses, dashing about town.

Two years later, the year World War One broke out, the McGill Ski Club was formed as an affiliate of the Montreal Club and some members, like Percy Douglas, took the train to Shawbridge every weekend to ski, although an increasing number of skiers at McGill and elsewhere were now in uniform. Still, enough skiers got away to the Laurentians that one of them decided it was high time to map some trails. Members of the Shawbridge Club who spend much time poring over ski maps are in the debt of Tom Drummond, a civil engineer, and the cousin of Huntly Drummond, an early Laurentian skier and champion jumper. Tom Drummond made his headquarters at Mrs. Marshall's boarding-house where, in 1916, he perfected an ingenious machine for mapping trails. It consisted of a bicycle wheel mounted between a pair of short skis equipped with a cyclometer and compass. Drummond on snowshoes pushed this contraption ahead of him, recording each turn of the wheel and translating this into miles as he tramped through the bush and over the hills along the Rivière-du-Nord from Shawbridge to Ste-Agathe and beyond. Many of Tom Drummond's maps, clear and precise and perhaps the basis for the skiers' pocket guide, the "Sweet Caporal Skiers' Book", graced the walls of Mrs. Marshall's boarding-house.

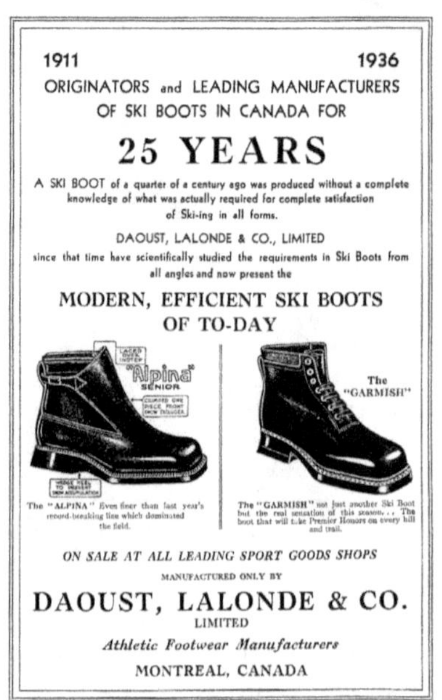

At this time, skiing meant flying down a hill, jumping and gliding through the snow. The skis themselves, seven-foot hickories, were still so heavy and clumsy that only the strongest skiers tried to climb a hill. The first poles were a flimsy affair, the bamboo shafts often splitting in the cold or the rings breaking and falling off. The original bindings were not much better – a toe strap and then a cane binding, sometimes with a seal skin for traction underneath the foot.

But help was on the way. Montreal's Daoust, Lalonde and Company located on Victoria Square, claimed they originated the first specially designed ski boots in 1912. And in Verdun, Mr. A. Palmquist was pushing "Norsh" ski wax made in Norway for thirty-five cents a bottle. Imagine what Mr. Birch would have done with that had he rubbed some onto his "Norse Snowshoes" thirty years earlier on his epic ski trip from Montreal to Quebec City.

But something had happened that would have a lasting influence on skiing both in equipment and style. Herman Smith Johannsen came to America.

"JACKRABBIT"

In 1894, at the age of nineteen, Herman Smith Johannsen graduated from Krigsskolen ("war-school") at Christiana – complete with plumed hat – as a lieutenant in the Royal Norwegian Army Reserve. Almost immediately, he went on to study engineering at the University of Berlin where he took his degree five years later. By this time, the man who would become the first honorary life member of the Shawbridge Club had been offered a job in Cleveland, Ohio, by the European representatives of a large industrial firm.

Alice and "Jackrabbit" in the Laurentians, 1934
(Peggy Johannsen Austin Collection)

So in December 1901, at the age of twenty-six, Johannsen sailed on the steamer, *Norge*, to seek his fortune in the new world. After a brief stopover in New York to see the sights and call at his new employers' head office, he hopped the train for Cleveland where he began work in the draughting department of Brown Hoist and Company, a large firm selling heavy equipment to railways, mines, the lumber trade and other resource industries.

By 1903, his English much improved, Herman received a raise and a promotion that entailed hitting the road to sell industrial equipment. Canada, where the railways were now pushing north and west, was one of his first assignments partly because, as he explained, none of the other salesmen were interested: "Nobody wanted to go to Canada. They thought it was full of bears walking the streets."

On this first trip "Jackrabbit" almost certainly skied in the Laurentians although he was not the first to do so. That distinction may well go to Cy Kennedy (later a founding member of the Shawbridge Club) who came up on the train after it reached Shawbridge and in 1901 was known as "the youngest skier in the Laurentians". On this first trip, Smith Johannsen ranged far and wide through northwestern Quebec. Later he would travel to the Lac-St-Jean area where in the company of Sir William Price and a number of other businessmen, he reconnoitred the Price Brothers' timber limits.

Normally, he would take the train to the end of the line, transfer to a horse and sleigh, and finally reach his destination by dogsled or on skis. It was on his first trip in the North Bay area that "Jackrabbit" met the Cree for the first time, a people with whom he made friends easily and whose honorary chief he would later become. The Cree, who used snowshoes to hunt and attend their trap lines, marvelled at Herman's varnished skis (lighter and smaller than the skis people used in Montreal), much faster than their own means of winter travel. It was "Jackrabbit's" first experience of skiing in Canada, a love affair that would last for the next three quarters of a century.

Herman and Alice with Ken in the Adirondacks, 1927

(Canadian Ski Museum Collection)

Only the year before while Johannsen was working in Cleveland, a love affair of a different kind began. In the winter of 1902, a mammoth blizzard paralyzed the city. Happily, "Jackrabbit" strapped on his skis and headed out on the snow-packed streets. Topping a small rise, he noticed beneath him a group of young people skating on a pond. He skied towards them and the skaters stopped to look at the bizarre "boards" attached to his feet. One of the prettiest girls exclaimed, "What fun that must be! Where did you learn to do that?" "Well," replied Herman, "she-ing is what we always do back home. It's the only way to travel in winter."

The young skater, a kindergarten teacher named Alice Robinson, was suitably impressed and, under Herman's gentle courting, this first impression turned into love. He and Alice (who with their children would also become members of the Shawbridge Club), were married on June 29, 1907. Alice, aged twenty-five, was seven years younger than her husband. They spent part of their honeymoon in the Adirondack Mountains in upstate New York.

Before his marriage, Herman had concluded that Brown Hoist was not as progressive a company as he had thought so he signed on briefly with another firm, then took off on his own and tried to establish himself as an independent "manufacturer's agent", selling industrial equipment for several firms.

This was his situation when, shortly after their wedding, Herman brought his bride along for her first visit to Montreal. (Of course, "Jackrabbit" himself had been in Montreal on various occasions selling heavy equipment to the Canadian Pacific Railway, even joining the

Montreal Ski Club in 1905.) One of the highlights of the trip was their apprehension at taking the quivering cable car to the lookout atop Mount Royal where they gazed on the panorama of the whole city at their feet and took each other's snapshots.

Telemarking at Lake Placid, 1921 (Canadian Ski Museum Collection)

The next few years were spent far from the snows of Montreal in Cuba, where Herman had often travelled in his early days with Brown Hoist. However, after the birth of their first child, Alice, in Havana on April 11, 1911, and because of Herman's recurring malaria attacks, they decided to pull up stakes and relocate in New York City. But New York proved to be a struggle and soon there would be two more children, Peggy and Robert. Herman was fed up. "Enough of this," he told Alice, "I can't stand this rat race any longer. What I need is to find a place where ... I can earn a living and also continue to live."

So Herman turned his business over to his brother, Otto, and packed up his family for the move to Lake Placid in upper New York state where they had already spent summer holidays. Ultimately, they hoped to move to Montreal, a city with which Herman was already familiar. He had kept a post office box there since 1919 and in 1922, shortly after the move to Lake Placid, he set up a new office in the Keefer building in Montreal and took a small apartment on Bishop street. He would do as much business as he could in Montreal, commute on the weekends to Lake Placid and find time to ski both in the Adirondacks and the Laurentians.

By the early Twenties, "Jackrabbit" knew a lot about the Laurentians where he had skied at every opportunity from the time he first visited Canada in 1903 selling heavy equipment for Brown Hoist. His return to business in Montreal coincided with a post-war boom in skiing. As Percy Douglas writes optimistically in *My Skiing Years,* "Gone are the days of snowshoes and toboggans, for skiing is now the king of winter sports in Old Montreal."

There were several reasons for this skiing boom. An expanding Montreal played havoc with the old ski areas in the city and snow conditions favoured the Laurentians. The horrors of World War One were past and soldiers wanted to climb out of the trenches and breathe fresh air again. There was more money to go around, sporting equipment was becoming more efficient, and so was transportation.

Trains now travelled farther, made more frequent departures and were jammed with skiers who boarded at Montreal's Mile End station, stashing their poles between the backs of their seats where they were held upright by small leather straps. They would usually get off at a higher station like Ste-Agathe and ski back down, sometimes as far as Shawbridge, where they'd catch the train home.

Even in the early Twenties, the trains thundering into the Laurentians were still enough of a novelty that the villagers turned out en masse to see them arrive, whistles blowing, bells clanging, in a cloud of hissing steam. Lucy Paré, a splendid skier herself, with a holiday house in Val-Morin, describes the scene in her wonderful memoir, *The Life Story of a Matriarch*:

Ski Train near Morin Heights, c. 1940 (CNR Collection)

"Habitants, farmers, lumberjacks, woodsmen ... seemed to make it their business to crowd the station platform and gape at newcomers arriving on the train. It was the biggest and only happening of the day in those isolated backwoods."

She remembers that it would take more than a day to reach Val-Morin from Montreal by car in the summer. Of course, there were no highways in those days and the roads, impassable in winter, sometimes just muddy tracks in the other seasons, were still primitive: "There was no direct route and one had to follow a series of 'chemins de rang', roads running in a zig-zag pattern along the borders of the various farm properties".

In fact, there is some evidence that, despite the rugged conditions, cars had made an earlier appearance in the Laurentians. In the summer of 1914, a couple of farmers reported that two or three of these gas machines appeared suddenly in a cloud of dust on the St-Hippolyte road, scaring them and their cattle.

But it was still by train that, in 1922, the Montreal Ski Club made their annual and, as it turned out, their last visit to the Manitou Club, where they had skied so often in the rolling wooded country around the lake near the village of Ivry where wealthy Montrealers had built their holiday homes and where the first French-speaking ski club, Le Club de Ski Mont-Royal d'Amérique, was founded by a Canadian sports enthusiast, Champlain Provencher, in 1917. None of the Montreal skiers had any idea it would be their final visit to the Manitou Club nor, I suspect, did they know all that much about the history of the Club and the splendid Laurentian property it dominated.

THE REMITTANCE MAN

The remarkable story of the Manitou Club property goes all the way back to 1891. In that year Madame la Comtesse Ogier d'Ivry of Chaîne-de-Coeurs, Le Mans, France, bought hundreds of acres around Lake Manitou – called "the Manitou farm" – from Benjamin A. Testard de Montigny, a prominent Montreal judge and author who was the Dean of the Canadian Zouaves, the military force sworn to defend the Papal states.

How in the world would a woman of the French nobility ever have heard about a property deep in the Laurentian wilderness? Almost certainly, she heard about it from the indefatigable Curé Labelle who, when he travelled to France in 1890 seeking emigrants, was toasted as the "Lion of Paris" and caught Madame la Comtesse's attention. But why on earth would she buy so remote a property? She did so for her second son, Viscount Raoul d'Ivry, to whom she would regularly send sums of money. In a word, the Viscount was a "remittance man". The phrase has a negative connotation, "the black sheep" of the family, but it need not be understood in that fashion. French law mandated that the first-born male, the Count, would inherit the family estate and was obligated to provide for his siblings. This often led to considerable quarrelling and tension – even in extreme cases, murder – so the family often thought it advisable to get the second son, the Viscount, off the scene.

Viscount Raoul D'Ivry

In any event, the Comtesse bought the extensive domain, helped her son build a magnificent chateau in the French style, and he and his wife and children took up residence in 1892, the very year the railroad reached Ste-Agathe, only a few miles from the shores of Lake Manitou.

Raoul was an enterprising and romantic young man in his late twenties. He was also an adventurer who put his hand to a series of endeavours, such as opening two sawmills, where he prospered for a time cutting hardwood trees. His other projects included mining, building houses near Ivry, the hamlet later named for his family, running a steamboat for summer visitors and operating a cheese factory. Sadly, the mining did not pan out, the lumbering and the cheese factory lost money, and the passenger steamer caught fire and burned.

It wasn't that Viscount d'Ivry was unwilling to have a go. The problem was that he tried too many things and was something of a dilettante. Besides which the Viscount had other interests. His splendid chateau, high on a hill overlooking the lake, was a party house where he loved to entertain. And he was a party animal so that, whenever he received his remittance money, he would head straight for the bar in Ste-Agathe and buy rounds of drinks for his cronies. As a result, poor Raoul was often in debt to the local tradesmen and farmers.

The Manitou Club (John Cushing Collection)

The Viscount had many friends around the lake because he himself was a convivial soul. In many ways, he was a hail fellow well met. He liked the high life. He had a sense of fun and more than a touch of class. At Christmas, he and his wife would send cards embossed with his family's gold crest. Often they walked through Ste-Agathe acknowledging their friends with a graceful bow. The Viscount was tall and slender with a distinguished air and a high-pitched voice. His wife was cultured and petite. They made an engaging pair.

But eventually the Viscount's business failures and profligacy caught up with him. About the turn of the century, he sold his magnificent chateau to a group of wealthy Montrealers, some of whom had lake properties, who were looking for a clubhouse for the Manitou Club.

Happily for Raoul, the proceeds from the sale gave him enough for a second start. He proceeded to build a large stone house on the shores of the lake near Ivry. Ethel Cushing (later a member of the Shawbridge Club) was one of those who knew him in this period and she remembers the

The Manitou Clubhouse, 1905
(Notman Photographic Archives, McCord Museum of Canadian History, Montreal)

Viscount as a rather eccentric person: "He spent all his money and built this beautiful enormous stone home but then he sold it. I remember him distinctly. He was tall, slight, quite good-looking but he did the most peculiar things. He used to take pot shots at ornaments and things that were up on the mantel over the fireplace."

World War One brought out the Viscount's romantic sensibilities. Just before hostilities broke out, he bought a big inboard motor boat for cruising the lake. But when his son, Gaétan, left to serve in France, Raoul vowed he would not use the boat until his son returned. According to George Mitchell, in his booklet, *Heritage Daldurn*, the son never returned so his father sold the boat to a Mr. Thomas Arnold, a wealthy homeowner on Lake Manitou.

Skiers near the Manitou Club (Overing Family Collection)

The Viscount's last home, a ramshackle one, on a knoll overlooking the train station at Ivry (incorporated in 1912), dramatically revealed his straitened circumstances. Gwen Marler Harris, whose family had a recreation home on Lake Manitou, remembers going by boat with her mother about 1940 to visit the Viscount and his wife: "They were both living in this home that was not much more than a shack. The remarkable thing was they were so cheerful and hospitable and had lost nothing of their gracious manners. They served us tea and I seem to remember the Viscount spilled his drink of Scotch. Of course, by this time, the remittance money had run out." In his declining years the Viscount was often seen happily working in his garden with a pick and shovel, oddly appropriate for a nobleman whose family crest displayed a pick crossing an axe.

Meanwhile, the group of well-to-do Montrealers, summer residents at Lake Manitou, had the clubhouse they wanted – a grand building with a European cachet in which to recreate, drink and dine and bed down after another day in the bracing Laurentian air. The Viscount's old home was to be an all-year-round club (Percy Douglas and his friends first skied there in 1905) but at first the emphasis was on summer sports, swimming, sailing and regattas. Snowshoeing was more popular than skiing which did not take off until after the war.

Sadly, all this came to a sudden end in 1922 when the Viscount's splendid old home burned to the ground. It says something for this beautiful property that the Canadian Pacific Railway purchased it in 1923 apparently with plans for a vast recreational development. However, a short time later, the Railway switched this project to Montebello near the Quebec-

Ontario border, perhaps because that location was accessible by yacht as well as by road and rail, and this new resort was called the Seigniory Club (now the Montebello Club).

In any event, shortly afer they recovered from the shock of their clubhouse burning down, some members of the Manitou Club, especially those who were keen skiers, sat down to discuss where they could find a new location. But that is another story.

Lake Manitou with Club at left (Overing Family Collection.)

THE BEGINNINGS

Not surprisingly, a few members of the Manitou Club, casting about for a new home, looked south towards Shawbridge, "the gateway to the Laurentians". They had often skied in the area, putting up at Mrs. Marshall's boarding-house. "Jackrabbit" himself told his family about the region from Shawbridge to Ste-Agathe "where one could ski from one village to the next, crossing through farm fields, climbing over fences, winding through maple groves, 'bushwhacking' through the forest beside a quiet lake, and finally coming down to the next town."

Shawbridge from the Big Hill, 1932
(Drysdale family Collection)

Alice, "Jackrabbit's" eldest daughter, describes in her excellent biography of her father, *The Legendary Jackrabbit Johannsen*, her very first ski near Shawbridge: "... Dad and I continued to pick our way across lakes and fields and fences until we arrived, just as darkness was falling, at the crest of the Big Hill at Shawbridge. From the summit, the North River Valley lay spread out below us, and the lights of the little village winked a welcome. Beyond, the hills blended softly into twilight, and above, the first stars began to glimmer. We took a long look. 'This is such a cozy, friendly country,' said Dad reflectively. 'I think I could comfortably live here for the rest of my days.'"

The village of Shawbridge itself was typical of hamlets in the north country. It is named after William Shaw who came out from Ireland in 1827, a member of the large Shaw clan that includes the immortal George Bernard himself. William married Martha Maria Mathews and they are considered the founders of Shawbridge in 1840. Other Irish and Scottish immigrants joined them so that by 1843 the census shows fifty-two "colonizers" living in Shawbridge, then called Mount Pleasant.

Travel at that time was an ordeal. The primitive "roads" had no gravel and were little more than a trail with two ruts that turned into mud during the spring and summer rains. The only way to do any serious travel was by horse and a conveyance. William Shaw and Martha Maria would usually get out of their wagon or buggy and walk behind to lighten the load.

Gradually, in the latter part of the nineteenth century, industries began to develop. Sawmills sold ties to the Canadian Pacific Railroad which had reached Shawbridge in 1890. The clay, thin and anemic, was not much good for farming but it was just right for making bricks so brick yards sprang up. Gordon Shaw, a genial one-eyed man who has lived all his life beside the graveyard in Shawbridge, has never seen a ghost, and is a descendant of William, recalls that his father's uncle, Albert Shaw, had a cement mixer: "He scooped the clay out like butter and made bricks for the houses around Shawbridge." Of course by the time Gordon Shaw was eleven years old in 1923, the year of the founding of the Shawbridge Club, where he was helping with the sleighs and horses to meet the trains, the railroads were carrying almost 10,000 skiers north in a season. Shawbridge, "the cradle of skiing in the Laurentians", had become a winter tourist town.

(Canadian Ski Museum)

The small group looking to replace the Manitou Club knew exactly what they wanted – the Stephens' farm and boarding-house on Rue Principale (later highway 11) between the Canadian Pacific station and the Rivière-du-Nord. In all likelihood, some of them would have stayed there overnight on their skiing jaunts to Shawbridge.

In 1881, Joseph Stephens bought the property from Frederick William Scott who had owned it since well before 1867, when Scott took out a loan of a hundred dollars on the land and the buildings where he was already living. After several transactions within the family, the property came into the hands of Joseph's grandson. His name was Joseph S. and he owned the property until 1919, only four years before the Shawbridge Club acquired it.

It was likely during the ownership of Joseph S. that the rambling farmhouse was turned into a boarding-house with bedrooms added onto the second storey and a spacious lounge with a fieldstone fireplace extending beyond the ground-floor kitchen. In 1914, G. Denton Lewis, who later became president of the Shawbridge Club, stayed in the Stephens' boarding-house with his mother as did other skiers who subsequently joined the Club.

Joseph S. Stephens kept cows, horses and goats on his farm but the spread was better known as a livery stable and a half-way station to board cattle overnight. Joseph had capacious barns behind his residence where he kept smart black carriages, shining buggies and handsome horses. The locals would marvel as the sleek horses pranced by, Joseph, wearing grey gloves and carrying a whip in his hand, seated on the postillion of the gleaming "express" carriage, taking four or five guests out for a ride before supper.

The Shawbridge Club (L.L.C. Collection)

Sometimes the Stephens' place was the scene of rougher excitement because it was also a stopover for the drovers and wranglers who brought horses and cattle down from further north on their way to sales in the stockyards of Montreal. Often, the "cowboys" on horseback, wielding their whips, had a hard time keeping the steers, cows, bulls and horses safely in their make-shift pens. The bulls would start to butt and brawl, adding to the dusty excitement.

The wranglers would say you had to watch out for highwaymen on the roads around Ste-Thérèse and, indeed, there was still an element of the frontier and the make-do about Shawbridge. In the early Twenties, the Kanienkahers, the Amerindian "people of the flintstone", still appeared along the shores of the Rivière-du-Nord. And, in a forerunner to one-stop shopping, Gordon Shaw remembers "when you were getting your groceries at the general store, you could get your teeth pulled at the same time."

On April 14, 1921, Joseph S. Stephens sold his farm and boarding-house to Marie Eugénie Lanctôt, the wife of his only son, Samuel A. Stephens, a manufacturer who listed his principal address as Lynn, Massachusetts. The selling price was three thousand dollars. Less than two years later, Samuel Stephens would become one of the founding members of the Shawbridge Club.

Sometime in the summer of 1922, a short time after the Manitou Club burned to the ground, the consortium that came together to acquire a new ski club leased the Stephens property from its owner, Marie Eugénie Lanctôt Stephens. This group that founded the

Shawbridge Club had several things in common. Many, but not all, were active skiers; most were reasonably well-off; about half had been members of the Manitou Club and either had summer residences at Lake Manitou or in Como. Many became heavy hitters in Montreal's business community. About half were on the higher rungs of investment companies, one would become president of the Montreal Stock Exchange and two would become corporate presidents. One would go bankrupt and another, reportedly, committed suicide because of financial losses.

Wilson Mellen, Betty Henderson standing and other early members, 1926

(Peter Mellen Collection)

Outside business hours, some of the group palled around together, especially those who had their roots in Como where they would arrange to go duck hunting together. Once one of them, a bit tipsy even in the early morning, fired his shotgun and accidentally killed all the live decoys. They played hard, worked hard and they were successful at what they did.

That was the group, then, who shelled out fifteen dollars each in 1922 to launch the Shawbridge Club. The legal name of the Club, which received its letters patent on March 13, 1924, was the Laurentian Lodge Club, Inc., but most of the earlier members and many even today refer to it by the more familiar name, the Shawbridge Club.

Members began to join immediately but for the first winter, while structures and furnishings were being put in place, they boarded with the Stephens. On January 5, 1923, the first signature appeared on the guest book. It was that of W. E. Macfarlane, followed by H. P. Thornhill and H. G. Welsford.

As for the building itself, one of the Club's most popular early members, Allan Turner Bone, who wrote an informative history of the Club's first fifty years, called it "the ugliest building in the Province of Quebec." No doubt this description related to the colour scheme, a curdled cream set off by the posts on the spacious wraparound verandah, so garishly painted with stripes of red and green, they resembled the poles in front of a barbershop. The original farm boarding-house of the Stephens, with so many appendages added on, had grown in a topsy-turvy fashion. And that's how the furnishings of the new Club were obtained, higgledy-piggledy.

Most furniture was bought second-hand at auction in Boston. Perhaps that was at the instigation of a founding member, Samuel A. Stephens, who resided in Massachusetts. The original beds, however, were purchased from the Montreal General Hospital for three dollars each. It was reported the hospital got rid of them because they were so uncomfortable it was impossible for even an unconscious patient to sleep in them. The new house committee tried to smooth out the lumps using brown wrapping paper which invariably snapped, crackled and popped at night whenever the incumbents moved, for whatever reason. The most impressive of the furnishings, a tall varnished grandfather clock, donated by the Birks family of Montreal, still dominates the lounge more than seventy-five years later. It is the only item remaining from the Club's early days.

N.M. "Mac" Yuile, first president, 1923 - 1929

(L.L.C. Collection)

The first president of the Shawbridge Club was N. M. "Mac" Yuile, the president of Cassidy's, a firm selling fine china in Montreal. "Mac" Yuile was one of the first half dozen to talk about a new Club in the summer of 1922. Another was Percy Douglas. Yuile was a strong competitive skier himself and in the fall of 1923, he put the Club on a sound financial footing and increased the number of members from thirty-four to eighty-two.

Percy Douglas, an original member

(Barbara Douglas Tindale Collection)

The Club was fortunate in the experience of its early members, many of whom had begun their skiing some years before in Montreal and elsewhere. One of these was Percy Douglas who, it was later said, was "part of every major ski development in Canada" – prominent member of the Montreal Ski Club, editor of *The Canadian Ski Annual*, in 1920 organizer and first president of the Canadian Amateur Ski Association and champion skier. After the fire at the Manitou Club, he writes that the Laurentian Lodge Club, the first residential ski club in the Laurentians, "was formed ... by a group of us, all interested in cross-country touring, who wished to have a conveniently located house for the weekends."

Right from the outset in the winter and spring of 1923 (when Toronto broadcaster, Foster Hewitt, excitedly shouted for the first time, "He shoots! He scores!"), the Shawbridge Club developed a certain dash and élan that reminded one member of the "the espirit de corps and camaraderie in an officers' mess." Of course, he was onto something especially as ladies could not appear except as guests of gentlemen members. But there was a comradeship because so many of the early members had fought in the war and distinguished themselves doing so. Eric Kippen, Mostyn Lewis, Lindsay Hall, Gordon Hanson, General Edouard de Bellefeuille Panet, who would become the Club's first French-Canadian president, and the Wallis brothers to name a few.

Maj. Clyde Drew (fourth from left) with some of his cohorts on the grounds of the club

"Dad was a machine gun officer at the Battle of the Somme with Col. Meighen's Canadian Grenadier Guards."

(Diana Drew Togneri Collection)

Hugh Wallis, also a Club member, writes of the two brothers: "Both my dad, 'Hal', and my uncle, Hugh, would tell stories by the hour in front of the fireplace, with their Scottish sense of humour. There were stories about those dirty filthy vermin-ridden trenches at Vimy and Passchendaele, and wonderful stories of heroism." These men and others had fought in the trenches of Europe, at Passchendaele and the Somme. The Battle of Vimy Ridge, where Canada came of age, only six years before, was not yet in the history books. What was the spirit they brought from the trenches, the seas and the skies and transmitted, at least in part, to the Shawbridge Club?

In his splendid book, *Vimy*, Pierre Berton writes: "Vimy stood for more than a war; it also stood for Canadian ingenuity, Canadian dash and daring, Canadian enterprise. The men who fought at Vimy weren't bland or boring. The techniques that won the battle were innovative. The men went over the top, knocking out machine gun nests, and sweeping the trenches of enemy gunners ... a certain élan ... there was a family feeling in the Canadian Corps."

Dash and daring, ingenuity, enterprise, innovation, a certain élan, family feeling. Is it an exaggeration to say the veterans who joined the Shawbridge Club brought some of those qualities and that spirit with them? I think not. They brought it, as Hugh Wallis says, with their Irish and Scottish sense of humour, sitting in the lounge beside the fireplace sipping their drinks and swapping their stories and they brought it to the ski hills. It was the spirit of the Wallis brothers and of Eric Kippen with his sonorous voice, craggy Spencer Tracy face and hooked nose, and of all the others as well.

Why did men of this calibre join the Shawbridge Club in the first place? It had no special cachet, the beds squeaked and the showers leaked. Why not join a prestigious club where you sank into leather chairs, unfolded *The Times*, and leaned back while the uniformed barman brought you a drink? Precisely, I think, because these men sensed there was still something of the frontier spirit in the mountains. They didn't want to lean back and go slack. They still sought challenges and they found them skiing the Laurentians.

(Overing Family Collection)

THE FLAPPERS

Tango in the Twenties: Mr. Vachon and dancing partner, Montreal, 1928 (Notman Photographic Archives, McCord Museum of Canadian History, Montreal)

As they sat in the lounge beside the crackling fireplace in the Club's first winter, 1922-23, the members swapped war stories but, in a lighter vein, chatted about the Montreal scene.

It was a lively one. Jackie Beaudoin Ross, later a Club member, who was until recently a curator at the McCord Museum, notes that "Tutumania" was sweeping the city at the time because of the discovery of King Tutankhamen's tomb in Egypt on November 26, 1922, an event thoroughly covered by the Montreal press:

"Adaptations of Egyptian-style clothing, furniture, and jewelry were spotted at many events. Mrs. Raymond Caron purchased a diadem in the Tutankhamen style in New York City and wore it to a ball at the Ritz in 1923. A theatre in the Egyptian style was built on Sherbrooke Street and still stands today." (The Cinema V building on Sherbrooke Street West.)

Other events also fuelled the conversation and gave the Roaring Twenties in Montreal their own distinctive flavour: "Jazz was much in the air. Paul Whiteman, the king of jazz, performed 'Rhapsody in Blue' at the St-Denis theatre shortly after the Club was incorporated. The well-known bar, Rockhead's Paradise, was jumping in the Twenties and featured local jazz.

"Among the young, lifestyle was excruciatingly fast, perhaps a recompense for lost years during the war. Hair was daringly shingled, makeup was brazenly worn and skirts abruptly crept upwards to the knee. The flapper was born – so-called because she rakishly wore her outdoor boots unbuckled so that they flapped! Shockingly, women smoked, often puffing away on glamorous imported Turkish cigarettes.

"The cocktail was invented and ladies could now be seen unabashedly drinking them in public. However, we are told that teetotalers protested, especially in Westmount! On the other hand, Shawbridge Club member, Michael Drummond's mother, remembers it was her husband who introduced the cocktail to her own family. Dances like the Charleston were fast and furious and entertaining. On November 15, 1924, Percy Cowans gave a Fancy Dress Ball at the Mount Royal Hotel for a thousand guests. Some Montreal skiers, like Dorothy Cook, travelled overseas by luxury liner to ski at St. Moritz and other European resorts. And one could now fly. The Montreal Light Aeroplane Club at St-Hubert was founded in 1927, and in its first exciting year 1,700 Montrealers applied for membership. Unfortunately, the early years of the sport saw a number of fatal accidents, including that of a well-known Montreal amateur pilot, John C. Webster. Yet, on their honeymoon in 1927, Michael Drummond's parents were brave enough to fly from Paris to London.

C.F. Sise, President of Bell Telephone Company, at the wheel on Peel Street (Michael Drummond Collection)

"And there was the automobile," concludes Jackie Beaudoin Ross, "which became increasingly popular in the Twenties. Sleek automobile shows proved a great attraction. Mrs. Drummond tells us that she personally witnessed Mr. Dandurand, purported to be the first owner of an automobile in Montreal, proudly driving down Sherbrooke street."

(Photo-Côté Collection)

In fact, as far back as 1898, City Alderman Ucal H. Dandurand, appeared on the streets of Montreal in a steam-driven car (called "a flying kettle") which he had purchased in Boston. Three years later, he bought a Dion-Bouton, "a gasoline buggy" for $1,535.00, a substantial sum at the turn of the century. Its wheels were large, its springs protruded, it had a goose-necked horn with a rubber bulb attached to it, carriage lamps and possibly a collapsible umbrella. Alderman Dandurand was suitably belted and booted – leather cap, pea jacket, gauntlets, goggles and a cotton duster.

In 1924, the Canadian National Railway announced that the dining cars on its transcontinental trains would be serving buffalo tongues and tails while the Montreal Canadiens began their first season playing in the new Forum by defeating Toronto's St. Pat's.

In the spring, the Club held its first sugaring-off party, the skiers standing in the woods in the sunshine eagerly rolling the fresh syrup in a bed of snow to make the delicious *tire*. Percy Douglas describes the joys of spring skiing in the Club's early days: "In late March when Montreal streets were bare of snow and the water running down the gutters, and on Mount Royal only the occasional snow remaining on the northern slopes, then it was that we ski enthusiasts enjoyed the finest skiing of the year in our beautiful Laurentians.

"The sun was burning hot pouring down from a cloudless blue sky ... Sleeves are rolled up, shirts opened at the neck, caps and gloves put away .... The mid-day lunch eaten at the summit of a favourite hill, with a panorama of mountains, lakes and valleys spread below; a rest and a smoke in the shady lee of a huge Laurentian boulder as old as the centuries themselves; the visits to the sugaring camps, and the refreshing drink of ice cold sap, from the tin bucket hanging on the maple tree ...

"The wood road leading down to Shawbridge was in grand condition ... and we had a rare run down into the village. The river was open, so we took off our skis and crossed on the CNR trestle, and ended up the season with our own excellent supper at the Shawbridge Club ..."

Two events in the early years disturbed this serene picture slightly. The Club's basement caught fire but was promptly put out by the manager, Mr. Harding, and Welsford and Wallis, a couple of early-rising veterans. However, the fire almost destroyed two engagements. Two young women sleeping at the Club could not believe that their fiancés, staying across the road in the Bachelor House, had not rushed over to save them from death by incineration. The big Montreal earthquake in the winter of 1927 rattled the dishes in the dining room but some of those partying in the upstairs rooms didn't even notice. At this time, the Club did not yet have its licence for alcohol so members brought their own liquor with their names written on the bottles.

Fletcher's Field c. 1925 (Archives Nationales du Québec, Centre de Montréal)

In his Montreal Guidebook for 1924, Charles Stokes testified to the growing popularity of skiing when he wrote: "Skiing might be said to have become the winter substitute for golf. Not very long ago it was the source of much merriment: there was something rather ridiculous in the spectacle of a grown man sliding around on long strips of wood! But no other winter sport now competes with it for popularity."

There were some keen golfers at the Shawbridge Club, none more so than W. C. McAllister, a tall aristocratic man who held himself like a plantation owner, and pushed hard to establish a golf course for the use of the members after the ski season was over. The land for the course, leased from the Clark Farm adjacent to the skiers' club house, saw the first players tee off in the summer of 1926. Only two holes were ready for play and often foursomes had to wait for the Clark cows to move before hitting their drives. Nevertheless, the Shawbridge Golf and Country Club was incorporated in 1927.

The annual lease for the golf course land, payable in two installments, amounted to $480.00. Golfers paid a small fee to become members of the ski club. Leigh Harding, the first manager of the winter club and a keen golfer himself, solicited new summer members, made bedrooms available for golfers and their guests, catered their meals and made everyone feel at home. At this early stage, there was considerable overlap between the memberships at both clubs. Allan Turner Bone always celebrated Thanksgiving en famille with a round of golf followed by a turkey dinner at the Club. (In those days the Shawbridge Club was open seven days a week year-round.)

Edna Ross was a keen skier who used to go up regularly to play golf, on one occasion with unexpectedly bizarre results: "One day two of us were at the furthest tee near the woods just about ready to start. Suddenly, a row of thick bushes parted and an absolutely naked man appeared: 'Do you girls want any balls?' he inquired and immediately disappeared. When we recovered from the shock, it struck us as awfully funny. Of course, it wasn't something you told at the Club as an after-dinner joke."

Not unless you wanted to risk a raised eyebrow from the manager. Leigh Harding had been a sergeant in the army where he had been in charge of forty soldiers. He had come to the Club from his position as chef at the Shawbridge Boys' Farm, a famous institution for delinquent and homeless boys from the English-speaking community. (William Stavert, a member in the Thirties, recalls that he shut his eyes tight every time he passed the Boys' Farm for fear his parents would send him there if ever he got into trouble.)

The Shawbridge Golf and Country Club, 1930

(Collection Ville de Prévost)

The Club was fortunate to have Leigh Harding as its first manager. A genial, spectacled, overweight man reminiscent of your small town druggist, he knew everyone by name, telephoned members when there was a vacancy and always put a positive spin for inquiries from Montreal about ski conditions. His daughter, Natalie, remembers those early days at the Club with her father and her mother, Anne:

Ralph Gosselin (at wheel) with André Pelrine

(Natalie Harding Anderson Collection)

"The founders wanted an informal place where they didn't have to dress formally, although the rule was that women changed into tea dresses for four o'clock tea, served in the lounge, and the men put on ties and jackets for dinner. No other place was as simple as the Club; these were people who could have been members anywhere else. When I came back fifty years later, the same string was hanging from those bare lightbulbs in the bedroom ceilings. Only a small shade had been added.

"Even in winter, fresh flowers were put on the train from Hall's greenhouses in Montreal West. Mother would never have anything else on the dining room tables. There were white linen table cloths and serviettes every night. Dad did the cooking in the beginning. The famous brown bread was his recipe. Then he hired a cook, and a pastry chef, Arthur, who was quite often under the weather. Dad would step in when he had to."

Early on Mr. Harding hired an assistant, Harry Lawton, who came to the Club when he was fifteen and stayed for forty-nine years. "Harry Lawton was part of our family," writes Natalie Harding: "He had landed up at the Boys' Farm because he had no home of his own. He knew the likes and dislikes of every member, whether you wanted coffee or tea." Yvon Blondin, whose father and grandfather owned the farm next to the Club, writes that "Harry was very classy. You wanted to be like he was when you grew up – that was his image. There were always kids around him."

Sometimes, Harding and Lawton would sit around the kitchen table laughing about the uproar caused by Fred Le Gallée who used to deliver cases of soft drinks from Allen's Beverages on Western Avenue (now de Maisonneuve), in Montreal. The Shawbridge Club was his first stop on his way north and he would unload with

Snacks are prepared in the kitchen.

Harry Lawton and the famous brown bread

(May Buick Collection)

"The original recipe for 'Nova Scotia molasses bread' was in an old cookbook that Dad brought with him from the fishing village where he grew up. It was always in the kitchen at the Club."

Natalie Harding Anderson

much banging and crashing about 4:30 in the morning. There was more noise when Fred returned to pick up the empties at midnight. Some members were not amused.

A young guest, Katherine, writing to her father who was vacationing in Florida, gives a vivid picture of activities at the Club in 1927:

A run into St-Sauveur (Joan McKim Collection)

"We went last weekend up to Shawbridge, a great skiing centre in the Laurentians, to stay with quite a large party at the Shawbridge Club. Such a bully crowd and so informal and nice. Well on Saturday we skied around the nearby hills and in the evening all danced in our ski clothes.

"Sunday a long ski trip was arranged over the mountains to a hotel in St-Sauveur for lunch. We started about ten, a gorgeous winter's day, three feet of perfect snow and everyone in top form. We arrived after such an exciting trip, wonderful hills, lovely trails winding through the woods, over lonely little lakes, and ending up with a run into St-Sauveur down the biggest hill they say in the country.

"When we stood on the top the village looked just like a toy one, right at our feet, but really two full miles away. As long as I live I never shall forget the thrill of that mad run into the valley below, our eyes blinded by the blazing sun and the flying snow. The lunch was quaint but good – Habitant pea soup, pork, eggs fried in maple syrup, native wine and the most marvellous apple pie with more maple syrup on it. The boys had sent over their instruments and after we lay around on the big divan before the fire, sang songs and snoozed, too dead tired to move."

Back in Montreal after the bracing weekend, the younger crowd from the Shawbridge Club could dance at the Ritz-Carlton, Canada's self-styled premier hotel. There was supper dancing every evening of the week from ten until closing and tea dancing every Saturday from four-fifteen until six to Melody King's orchestra. So the Shawbridge Club, as did Montreal and the rest of the country, danced its way to the end of the Twenties – the end, too, of the flappers, borne along by the melodies of the good life in the city and on the slopes, buoyed as well by what seemed to be a strong economy. At this time when prohibition and segregation were riding high in the United States, Montreal was one of the most open and tolerant cities in North America, visited by many American tourists including a fair share of black Americans.

On September 29, 1929, the Club, which for the first six years had leased the building, now purchased it for $8,000.00 from Maria Eugénie Lanctôt, the wife of Samuel Alexander Stephens whose father had driven his guests for those genteel buggy rides before supper.

There was an air of optimism about, exemplified in the advice of Eaton's, the most trusted store in Canada: "Put wings of skis on your feet and ride the air like a Valkyrie." And if that were not enough, you were invited "after the Day's Sport to Dine and Dance at the Windsor Grill, 'The cosiest room in the city'."

The Windsor

ON

DOMINION SQUARE

MONTREAL

THE Restaurant business of The Windsor has been developed through its good foods and kindly disposed service ~ ~ ~ ~ ~

Dancing in the Grill during Dinner and Supper hours

D. B. MULLIGAN - - - *Vice-President & Managing Director*

(CPR Collection)

"ALL ABOARD"

On October 29, 1929, just a month after the Club purchased the Stephens' house, the markets crashed. P. B. "Banty" Reid, later a Montreal investment dealer and Club member, was in New York working for the Bank of Montreal at 64 Wall Street. On his way to work, he would see bankrupt bankers, brokers and investors selling apples on the street corners.

One morning he passed a man on the sidewalk covered by two dirty burlap bags. He had jumped from his office window. And when he arrived at work another day, all the talk in the office was about another man in the office tower just down the street who had jumped to his death, his body slicing through the wooden frame of a taxi killing the cabbie.

As we shall see, the world-wide financial meltdown and the ensuing Great Depression affected the Shawbridge Club. But, paradoxically, more skiers than ever were heading for the Laurentians. One reason was the rapid development of Montreal as a great city and the concomitant adverse changes in the city's snow conditions. But the main reason for the growth of skiing in the north was the increased number of "snow trains". In the winter season of 1927-28 alone, they carried 11,000 skiers to the Laurentians. In so doing, they created an exciting way of life for Montrealers eager to escape the rigours of winter in the city.

(CPR Collection)

Percy Douglas captures some of this excitement on a bright Sunday morning catching the train for Shawbridge at the early hour of 7:30:

"When we reach the Mile End Station of the C.P.R.'s mountain branch line, the taxis are discharging their loads of boys and girls, and every arriving street car adds its quota to the merry throng.

"Our special Sunday morning car is on the rear of the train and at nine sharp, we are all aboard and on our way. What a jolly crowd it is, mostly the younger set, pretty girls all in knickers and gay coloured sweaters, boys in every kind of costume, with here and there the regulation dark blue ski uniform marking some expert and an occasional older person to do the heavy chaperone act ...

"The bridge players settle down to their game, others read the Sunday Illustrateds or they talk and the hour and a half passes quickly and before we know it we are at our mountain station. (Some go on to Mount Rolland), the rest of us getting off at Shawbridge to play around the ski Club."

The excited skiers received a warm welcome at the Shawbridge station: "All the villagers turned out in force to see the trains coming in. There were no motor cars, but every kind of sleigh, with the air echoing the merry music of their bells. The residents were on snowshoes; every one was dressed in furs and talking away in French." The skiers heading for Shawbridge who had cars were invited to use them. The Royal Garage at the foot of McGill College had the formula, "For a more pleasant Sunday Ski Day. Drive down to the Station in your own car in the morning, leave it at the Royal Garage, then pick it up on the way in at night."

Skiing from the train at Piedmont (Blanchard family Collection)

Maxwell delivering members to the Club. Jack Rutherford standing (L.L.C. Collection)

So popular did the "snow" trains become that, after discussing his plan with fellow-members at the Shawbridge Club, Percy Douglas convinced his friend, Sir Percy Thornton, President of the C.N.R., to run the first ski trains (soon followed by the C.P.R.), a whole train with ancient wicker-seated passenger cars, especially for skiers.

The famous ski trains were the most popular means of transportation to the Laurentians until after World War Two. As members of the Shawbridge Club recall, half the fun was getting there by train. Herbert Lewis remembers catching the train on Friday night: "Montreal on a snowbound Friday, the trees heavy laden, the snowbanks enormous, my father Mostyn Lewis and myself skiing from our home at the corner of Argyle Avenue and Westmount Boulevard, down the hill to Westmount Station to catch the train north. We had all our gear on our backs in those early days, heavy and cumbersome canvas backpacks."

"The trains," writes Charlotte Millen, "were usually packed to the doors – a forest of skis upended between the seats, duffle bags in the aisles, pandemonium and good cheer everywhere. Some nights, the trains lost traction on the frozen rails and were often hours late, the air becoming thicker by the mile with a smokey build-up of congenial fug. As time went by, sleep or stupor stilled the racket until each hard-won station claimed its revellers with a wake-up shot of rarefied air."

General Edouard de B. Panet (with dog); Col. Eric Kippen and Marguerite Kippen; Reginald Plimsoll; Amy Heney; Natalie Harding; Dorothy Southam (Bruce Kippen Collection)

When the train reached Shawbridge, it was met by a red sleigh with the Club's name emblazoned on it, pulled by a handsome team of Percherons and driven by Gordon Maxwell, manager of the Clark farm and a carpenter who built some of the renovations at the Club. "It was wonderful," writes Anne Henry Murdoch, "to load our skis and knapsacks onto the sleigh and jump in to snuggle in huge buffalo rugs, listening to the bells on the horses' collars as we were driven up the drive and around to the front door."

Diana Drew Togneri has a slightly more pungent memory of the trip from the station with Maxwell: "We'd be picked up by horses and a sleigh, covered with smelly robes to set off for the Club, lurching through ruts along the unploughed road in the dark. Everything stank of horse sweat and manure. The horse would lift his tail and flecks of manure would fly over everything. No one bothered in the slightest. We are all so antiseptic nowadays."

More intrepid skiers would skip Maxwell's sleigh and ski or walk to the Club. Gerry Allen, an accomplished pianist, who still plays for sing-songs on a Saturday night, recalls the walk from the station: "Your boots would crunch on the snow. The stars were out and the air was clear." And occasionally the trains would let you down. Jane Lewis was the daughter of the first president, "Mac" Yuile: "I remember one New Year's Eve with the sleigh bells twinkling. We went up to stay with friends further north with the plan of returning to the Club by train. There was no train. Our friends said a horse and sleigh could bring us to St-Sauveur. So we walked down the railway track on New Year's Eve in the moonlight."

And there were times when members found the ski trains a hair-raising experience. Libby Leslie remembers her uncle, Jack Rutherford, on the eve of his wedding: "Uncle Jack was a member and he had planned his bachelor party in Montreal to be followed by a weekend at the Club. The party went off fine but the groom and his guests had to rush to catch the train which went only as far as St-Jérôme where they had arranged to meet Maxwell's sleigh drawn by the black Percherons. Because two of the party, Andy and Eddie Renouf, could not fit into the crowded sleigh, they valiantly rode horses in full formal attire including top hats, to the door of the Club."

Natalie Harding, the manager's daughter, couldn't get over how many different ways members arrived at the Club: "Some walked or skied from the trains. Frank Common was driven up by his chauffeur. General Panet had his own car at the end of the C.P.R. train; it was kept closed at the Windsor Station until all the Club members riding with the General had boarded. 'Clee' Dodge and his two sisters, with their Swedish governess, would arrive the day after Christmas on the sleeper from New York City.

"Bill Pollock had a small plane, single engine, open cockpit. One day, he came into land on the golf course, and the propeller broke off. The Pollocks stayed at the Club until a new propeller arrived from Montreal. My father displayed that propeller on the wall of his office until the day he left the Club."

Gordon Shaw remembers the generosity of some of those arriving by train: "I used to help Maxwell bring the skiers by sleigh to the Club. One of those who came up was Mr. Plimsoll [a descendant of Samuel Plimsoll, the British marine activist, who gave his name to the line on ships showing the water level]. He was wearing this big raccoon coat and a warm fur cap. I would carry his valise and put it on the verandah of the Club. I was ten years old [1924] and he gave me fifty cents. I could hardly sleep that night for excitement."

Orian Stewart tries to capture the magic of it all: "It was a real journey to get to the Club in those early days. First the train, then you were met by those lovely big horse-drawn sleighs, like something you'd see in the movies. In those days, lack of snow was never a problem. There was always plenty.

"It was a whole different world. The Club was one of the few places you could stay if you loved skiing. It was homey. It was a wonderful old Club and nobody seemed to mind its slightly ancient aspects. They were rather endearing."

THE NEW YORKERS

(Barbara Douglas Tindale Collection)

During the winter before the Depression hit, Percy Douglas' son, Chrystie, also a member, invited two of his friends from New York City to the Club for a weekend of ski-ing. Chrys Douglas had first met Corey Ford, a writer and American humorist, at Columbia University in the 1920s and Corey invited Percy Crosby, a well-known artist and originator of the cartoon, "Skippy".

This is how Corey Ford described what happened next in *The New Yorker* article entitled "Loads of Fun on Snow and Ski":

"The skiers' paradise," the rear flap of the Canadian National timetable dubbed it, "with its steep dazzling hills for the expert, and its gentle easy slopes for the timid tyro." (I didn't like that "timid tyro" attitude. It sounded a little patronizing.) "Shawbridge," it continued to gloat, "with its cold bracing air, mysterious blue shadows and infinite hills that seem to touch the very sky." (I suppose you do get that impression when you look down from one.) "Return at night," the timetable fairly chortled, "with rosy cheeks, sparkling eyes, and a feeling of fitness and exuberance with which to tackle the task on the morrow."

It was that last line that got us. We wanted to face the task on the morrow with a feeling of fitness and exuberance. We wanted a couple of sparkling eyes, and some rosy cheeks. We wanted cold bracing air, mysterious blue shadows and infinite hills; and so we decided to go to Canada for a weekend ski-ing trip. That was where we made our big mistake. It would have been cheaper just to have stayed home and fallen downstairs.

The clerk in the sporting-goods store said we needed heavy socks. Anybody who was going skiing in Canada needed heavy socks; and heavy gloves; and heavy pants; and a couple of heavy shirts. And heavy underclothes, of course. Plenty of heavy stuff, that was the secret of a good skiing trip. We finally staggered over to Grand Central that night with four suitcases filled with our skiing costume, in addition to a couple of heavy shirts which we had to wear because they wouldn't fit in the bags, our ski-boots knotted around our necks by the laces, a pair of thirteen-foot skis under one arm and a pair of ski-poles under the other, all of which caused considerable good-natured chaffing in Forty-second Street before we finally disappeared into the sanctuary of the sleeper. Well, let them snigger. Sour grapes, that was all. Sheer envy. Tomorrow they would still be bending over their desks in stuffy offices, while we were speeding down a couple of these infinite hills that seem to touch the very sky ...

New Yorkers Aboard! (CPR Collection)

Just enough time in Montreal to buy us each a skiing cap (a blue affair with a long vizor, like a coal miner gone collegiate) and a couple of bottles of Scotch and a little cognac, just as a precaution to tide us over Sunday in case it got cold skiing. And just enough time left to stop in Krausman's for one glass of ale before the train left. Wouldn't be Montreal without a glass of ale at old Krausman's, ha, ha. Some different from Danny's, huh? Have we got time for another?

"Boy!" I said, setting down the glass. "I can hardly wait to get out in that cold bracing air, and strap on the old skis –"

"Right up to the top of the mountain with us," said Percy. (As a matter of fact, his name is really Percy Crosby and I see no reason for calling him Bill or Ed just for this article.) "None of those sissie slopes for mine."

"I bet those chaps back home are envying us now," I laughed. "Have we got time for just one more?"

Chrys Douglas, our host, looked at his watch anxiously. Train left in ten minutes. So we grabbed time for just one or two more; and arrived breathless at Tunnel Station with our skis under our arms, just in time to see the rear platform disappearing up the track, and no train till the following

The New Yorkers missed the Big Hill

(Collection Ville de Prévost)

noon. A whole day to wait till we could get on skis! We weathered the blow like men, and with a sigh of resignation we went back to Krausman's for just one more.

That was Thursday; and Saturday afternoon, sure enough, we arrived in Shawbridge, skis and baggage and a slight throbbing headache behind the left temple. Pile out, everybody! Get a lungful of this cold bracing air. I bet the bunch in New Yo ... haugh ... haugh ... Into the sleigh, up the hill to the clubhouse, pile your bags in the room, and on with your duds. Out on the porch, Chrys rubbed his hands gleefully. Just time for an hour's skiing before supper!

I looked at Perc. He looked at me. To think of being on skis at last! To think of climbing the mountain this very evening! It was almost too much. In fact, on second thought, it was too much.

"Chrys," I explained as tactfully as possible, "thinking it over, we've decided it might be best if we spent the rest of today just more or less getting acquainted ..."

Chrys looked at us suspiciously. " ... you know, watching how it's done," I rushed, "getting used to this cold bracing air ..."

He kneeled and buckled on his skis in silence.

"... when we learn to ski," I continued, "we want to embark with the proper spirit upon what is without doubt the greatest sport in the ..."

Chrys shoved forward and coasted down the hill from the clubhouse alone.

"... because it is the greatest sport in the world," I maintained to Perc later, as we sprawled before the fire. "Just think of those saps bending over their desks in stuffy offices, instead of breathing this cold bracing air ..."

"'Solutely," nodded Perc, and filled another glass.

"It certainly will be good to get on those skis tomorrow," I added heartily.

"'Lutely," nodded Perc. "Shall we open this second brandy?"

It turned cold that night. We didn't notice it at first, because we spent most of the evening before the fire with some fellow-skiers from McGill University, arguing about Anglo-American relations. It was a very pleasant argument, and it ended with a handsome parade through the clubhouse, an impromptu speech by Perc on international amity, patriotic songs of both nations, and a rather ugly fist-fight in the front-hall; and when we finally turned in about four o'clock, Chrys was asleep. So we threw all the windows wide open and crawled under the blankets, and as a result the thermometer dropped to thirty-six degrees below by morning, and Chrystie froze his ear in bed. He was very nice about it, however; and when he returned after a morning's skiing and woke us up for lunch, he was as full of enthusiasm as ever.

"What's the thermometer now?" Perc inquired.

"Seventeen below," Chrys said. "In the sun," he added cheerfully.

So that afternoon, while Chrys was out skiing again, Perc and I sat around the fire and looked forward to the splendid skiing we would have tomorrow. Tomorrow we would show them some *real* skiing around here. Say, a cross-country trip to St. Sauveur, around by the lakes, and home again for supper. Or perhaps a few thrilling descents of the big mountain opposite, and the rest of the day brushing up on our telemarks and christies. It would be easy enough to learn.

"Just keep one foot a little in front of the other," I said. "That's the whole secret about skiing. And a little more soda in mine, if you please."

"You should keep the skis parallel, of course," Perc agreed. "It's funny they don't serve you ice here. I think it tastes flat without ice."

"And balance on your toes," I added. "Lean forward and rest your weight on your toes."

"By the way," said Perc, "you don't happen to have a little ice in your pocket, by any chance?"

"Bend your knees," I said, "and balance with your shoulders ..."

"I wonder what they'd say," Perc mused, "if I went out and got some snow."

A slight disturbance in the outside hall roused our attention.

"Sorry to trouble you." A face appeared in the doorway, smiling through a large patch of adhesive tape. "But do either of you chaps happen to have some arnica handy?"

"Hurt yourself?" we asked weakly.

"Oh, no," he laughed. "I did *this* last week – ran into a pine-tree, that was all – no, this is for my friend here. He just ran a ski-pole through his cheek."

"I s-saw some arnica in the bathroom," said Perc.

"Oh, *that* was all used up this morning," smiled the face. "Some chap got tangled up with the barbed wire on the big hill ..."

Perc poured himself another glass of brandy.

The next morning Chrys stuck his head in the doorway of the bedroom for a moment. "Bill and I are going cross-country in St. Sauveur," he explained briefly, "and we won't be back before supper. You'll find your skis right out in the hall, as usual," pointedly, "in case you want to put them on for a moment to take some pictures of each other."

He reappeared a second later in the window. "I've ordered you another case of ale," he added coldly.

They put us on the New York train Tuesday night, and we both vowed to Chrys as we left that it was the best weekend we had ever enjoyed. There is no sport like skiing, Perc and I agreed. There's no sport that gives you such rosy cheeks, sparkling eyes, and a feeling of fitness and exuberance with which to face the task on the morrow."

No doubt many a skier read about the Shawbridge Club when Corey Ford's vivid description of "the best weekend we had ever enjoyed" appeared on the pages of *The New Yorker* on February 16, 1929. And no doubt Chrystie Douglas kept his copy as proof that he, at least, had hit the slopes.

FOSTER'S FOLLY

Alex & Pauline Abrams Foster
(Karen Foster Collection)

The advent of the ski trains (by the end of the Thirties 325 trains were carrying 145,000 skiers a season) multiplied the number of skiers heading for the Laurentians. And as the decade began, another development – this one almost in the front yard of the Shawbridge Club – changed the nature of skiing itself.

The young man behind this second change was Alex Foster, a former McGill student, who had won the Dominion Ski Jumping championship while still attending Westmount High School. Karen Foster, Alex's daughter, says her father was called "the flying ski". "He couldn't dance a step but he was a ballerina on skis, very poised and balanced. He enjoyed every thing about the sport and what it might mean to other people."

Although he was six feet tall and weighed 200 pounds, Alex enjoyed doing acrobatics on skis and liked nothing more than racing down a hill at top speed, spumes of snow tailing him all the way. Perhaps, because of the weight he lugged around, he was less keen on trudging back up the hill for another run. Alex discussed the problem with "Jackrabbit" who, by the early Thirties, had organized ski training clubs in several Laurentian villages and towns. How, he wondered, could they save time climbing the hills so as to have more time to devote to downhill racing and slaloming?

Young Foster had a bent for tinkering and engineering and, after graduating from Westmount High in 1929 with his pal, Brodie Shearer, apparently he rigged up a wooden mock-up of a hill using cords for a rope tow, in the basement of the family home. About this time, too, Alex had been accepted on the Canadian ski team for the 1932 Winter Olympics at Lake Placid.. Team officials were not only taken with his incredible jumping but with his "freestyle", executing a series of fancy twirls. Sadly, a serious accident during the run up to the Olympics ended his Olympic career. "Instead of joining his team mates for a drink," his daughter Karen recalls, "he went up the hill for one last run, he fell and tore up his knee which the doctors, at first, wanted to amputate."

His knee gradually recovered but the accident left Alex time to concentrate on his home-grown experiments. In the winter of 1930, Foster, then almost twenty-two, constructed something resembling the model in his basement, near the bottom of the Big Hill in Shawbridge.

If you looked out from the front door of the Shawbridge Club, across the tracks and over the river beyond the trees, you would see the Big Hill covered with snow and indented part way up like a two-tiered, white wedding cake listing slightly to one side.

Foster's original construction involved hoisting an old car on blocks, removing a tire from one of the back wheels, running a rope up to a pulley attached to a tree or a stake, starting the car's engine and hoping for the best. There is no doubt that Alex Foster rigged up this contraption but there is considerable confusion about when he did it, the dates ranging from as early as 1929 to as late as the winter of 1933.

The Dodge in action

(Photo, W. R. Drysdale, Sally Drysdale Aitken Collection)

Perhaps much of this confusion stems from the fact that Alex Foster developed his tow at different times in two stages. One who had first-hand knowledge of this was Cleveland "Clee" Dodge, Jr., who in 1930 was eight years old. He describes his experience:

"In February, 1930, I travelled with my parents and my sister, Betty, to visit the Wilder Penfields in Montreal. Afterwards we joined the Schieffelins, the Fred Osborns and the Percy Douglasses at the Shawbridge Club.

"One day about the middle of February, we were out skiing near the Big Hill. I noticed two or three men who were mounting an auto chassis on large beams. They had mounted a pulley in the place of one of the rear wheels. A rope

Holding on tight (Photo, W. R. Drysdale; Sally Drysdale Aitken Collection)

was wound with several turns around the pulley. This rope was then extended up a smaller hill which was just north of the Big Hill.

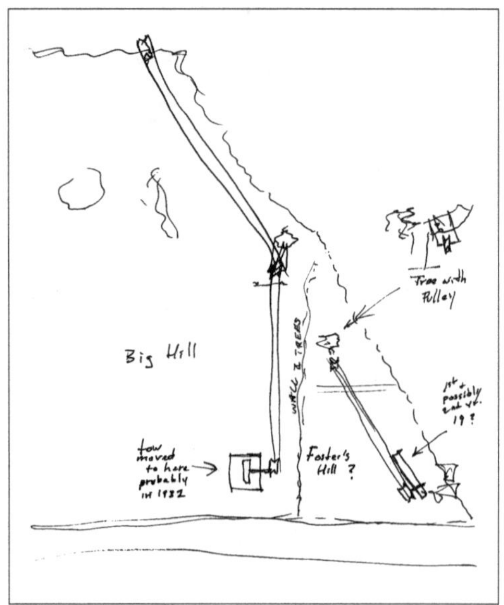

"Clee" Dodge's provisional sketch of "Foster's Folly"

"I remember coming down the road, probably after crossing the river on the rail bridge which we children were forbidden to use. Curious to know what was going on, I left the road and skied over to the auto chassis. At that moment the rope started to move slowly above the ground. I pointed my skis toward the hill and grabbed the rope with my gloved hands. The rope pulled me along the flat area just in front of the hill. I was only eight years old and I found the rope very heavy as I started moving up the hill so I let go and fell away from the rope.

"Having watched this performance, the men working on the auto chassis stopped the engine and turned their attention to improvements. I skied back to the road and went on to the Big Hill where I rejoined my companions and started the climb up the Hill.

"I had a mastoid operation the following fall so I did not visit the Shawbridge Club in the winter of 1931.

"But in January, 1932, I returned with my parents and the Schieffelins. We found that the ski tow had been removed from the smaller north hill and was now located on the Big Hill. It had been mounted along the fence and the row of trees which divided the two properties. A pulley had been mounted to turn the rope going up the Big Hill to the left so that it could continue on to the pulley at the top where it turned back down. I recall we had great difficulty with that turn at the half-way point because we were forced to let go of the rope before it went through the pulley. It was doubly difficult when our mittens froze to the rope and we had to pull them off our hands or the rope would take mittens and ski poles right through the pulley. For the same reasons, it was even more difficult to cope with the pulley at the top of the Big Hill.

"This time, January 1932, we questioned the operator of the rope tow, Mr. Alex Foster. He told us that the tow had been moved from the smaller hill

(Karen Foster Collection)

to the Big Hill in the summer of 1930 and that it had started operating in that location sometime between December, 1930, and January, 1931. At that time Mr. Foster started charging for the rides and the tow on the Big Hill became a commercial operation."

"It would seem the 1930 prototype, on which I had hitched a ride, demonstrated that ski tows would work. This prototype was then used as a working model to design the first commercial rope tow which operated spasmodically during the winter of 1931.

"Although it was a long time ago ["Clee" Dodge is now seventy-eight], I often told my family that I was the first person in the world to ride a ski tow and, indeed, I think I was."

So there would seem to be a natural progression from the prototype in the winter of 1930, on the smaller north hill to the Big Hill, where the first commercial tow began operating in January, 1931.

It was then, with some members of the Shawbridge Club looking on, that Alex Foster and a few of his pals jacked up a four-cylinder Dodge (used in the summer as the Shawbridge taxi) onto two low cement blocks, removed a rear tire, ran 2,400 feet of hemp rope around the tireless rim and up to the pulleys he had installed at the very top of the Big Hill, and started the Dodge's engine while the Club's skiers forked over their five cents and grabbed the rope as it jerkily began to move, not realizing perhaps, they were watching history before their very eyes.

And they were. This cumbersome contraption, soon dubbed "Foster's Folly", partly because, at five cents a ride or twenty-five cents for the day, it never broke even, is recognized as the first ski tow in the world. (Although funiculars and cable cars were used by skiers in Europe, they were not built as ski tows.)

Moïse Paquette's Aeroski, 1926 (Photo Coté Collection)

Foster's invention on the Big Hill in sight of the Shawbridge Club caused a revolution in skiing in North America, then in Europe. As Louise Arbique writes about his brain-child in her handsome book, *Mont Tremblant*, "No moment has been more crucial in the history of skiing."

Curiously enough, about the same time a garage owner in Ste-Agathe named Moïse Paquette was working on a similar tow on which he took out a patent in 1935.

Still, as members of the Shawbridge Club soon discovered, there were ups and downs to the world's first ski tow. Dr. Wilder Penfield's daughter, Priscilla, describes her experience taking the tow with her future husband, Bill Chester:

"We'd latched onto the tow to the left when the long knitted cuff of my old leather mitts twisted into the rope near the pulley at the top so I pulled my hands out! The mitts, still clutching my bamboo poles, went up through the wheels and were neatly dropped at my feet, looking like shredded wheat!" And this despite the warning Gordon Shaw remembers, "There was an open pulley at the top and you'd be warned – don't put your hand in that pulley or it'd come right off." Gordon Shaw worked on the tow almost from the beginning: "I had a big horse named Prince who weighed in at 1,500 pounds. I used to help Foster with that rope tow. One year they had a tent and restaurant at the foot of the tow at the bottom of the Big Hill. There was an anchor to hold the rope and a tightener."

Gordon Shaw remembers
(Vincent Thorburn Collection)

"They had the wrong kind of rope on that first tow," wrote Jane Lewis, daughter of "Mac" Yuile, the Club's first president. "Everyone came in with rope burns on their hands. It also collected water so that when you got to the end it was soaked." There were other hazards especially if you were on the small side as Bruce Kippen, then aged seven, remembers: "I would hang onto the tow for dear life with my feet dangling over the first gully as we chugged up the 'Big Hill'. The older people had their skis firmly on the ground but my legs were too short to reach."

Several of the youngest skiers developed their own ways of dealing with their shortness. Janice Bernabucci describes how she coped: "I would struggle up the Big Hill hanging on to that silly rope tow. The rope was so heavy that I always made sure there was a big burly guy right in front of me. That rope would dig a trench a foot deep in places when it came to one of those knobby moguls. I'd hang on for dear life while the guy in front lifted the rope. More than once I'd fall in a heap, laughing and giggling with all the people on the rope behind me."

Joan Fitzpatrick remembers how "we all struggled with that rope tow. It was just maddening to see Murray Hayes, later a halfback for the McGill Redmen, hanging onto that darn rope with one hand, swinging out sideways in an arc. It didn't seem fair." Andrea Burgess made a virtue out of necessity: "I was very light and small, and couldn't hold onto the rope tow, especially when it got so heavy in the spring, so I'd get on just behind Murray Hayes. That way, he'd be holding all the weight of the rope. One day, I made it to the top on my own. Was I proud? The main thing was that old tow worked, and it got you to the top."

Bruce Kippen says it didn't always work: "Half the time that rope tow was frozen and wouldn't start and the boys would all be standing around in the tent that covered the base of the hill pouring in anti-freeze for all they were worth. I didn't realize it at the time but I was seeing the founding era of downhill skiing before my eyes." Kenneth Hague recalls that "it was more necessary to have strong arms than strong legs to ski on the Big Hill.. Being lifted into the air by your armpit or having your knuckles dragged down into the icy ruts was exhausting."

Like his peers, Andrew Hugessen says the rope tow "was a hairy ride for a kid. First, the rope tried to grind you into the ground at the brow of the first rise, then, in the ensuing flat, it hoisted you aloft. The rope had this bad habit of twisting and trying to snag your sweater. We wore leather mitts with reinforced palms for gripping the rope but they seldom lasted more than one season." Bill Stavert has his own way of describing Foster's Folly: "It took several boys in a row to hold up the heavy wet rope and we were always careful to prevent the rope falling on our legs for fear of amputation, or getting our scarves wound in the rope for fear of being strangled by the pulley at the top."

(CPR Collection)

It's not surprising there was the occasional accident of one kind or another. Elizabeth Angus Eberts remembers "lacing up my old brown ski boots and trying to fasten my ski harnesses and then off through the field to the Big Hill. Once there, we had to climb the Hill – at the beginning it took me hours to get to the top, my skis coming off and sliding back to the bottom. Thank goodness, I was able to learn to use the ski tow. However, I remember one particular day going to the Big Hill, when I got stuck on a barbed wired fence trying to get to the Hill and left half my pants behind!"

Lillian Doyle describes how her daughter, Topsy Gillespie, fell into the snow at the top of the rope tow. "The heavy snow had also knocked down those power lines at the top of the Big Hill. When Topsy fell off the tow, she tumbled into the power lines and got a very exciting shock."

"It was a miracle if you made it to the top," writes Orian Hodgson. "If you fell, everybody behind you would land up sprawled down the Hill. But once you got the hang of it you could go up and down all day."

Skiers all over the world soon got the hang of it (the first ski-lift in the United States was installed in Woodstock, Vermont, in 1934). They went up and down all day and this development changed forever the nature of skiing so that Alpine racing at top speeds downhill gradually overtook the traditional Nordic or cross-country, in popularity.

So it was that Alex Foster, the Big Hill and, in some sense, the Shawbridge Club itself, were associated with the major turning point in the history of skiing in the twentieth century.

THE DIRTY THIRTIES

"Jackrabbit" with Ken (Canadian Ski Museum Collection)

Although he was an engineer and had discussed plans for the rope tow with Alex Foster, "Jackrabbit" Johannsen had reservations about this development. Not entirely in jest he would give this advice to his younger followers at the Shawbridge Club: "Get off those ski lifts, get off those crowded ski slopes, and get out in the bush on cross-country skis and enjoy this great country of ours." Or as Club member and author John Fry writes, "he would think it just as wrong for someone to use a lift to learn how to ski as he'd disapprove using a calculator to learn arithmetic."

Long before "the dirty Thirties", the "Chief" was out exploring the Laurentian countryside where the winter snows had never been marked by a ski track. His face tanned, lined and weather-beaten by the wind, he could ski fifty miles in a day over rough terrain. Sometimes he had a rifle slung from his shoulder to shoot deer which Alice would transform into char-broiled venison steaks, marinated and oozing with tangy juices.

Usually on these jaunts (some would last several days), "Jackrabbit" was accompanied by Ken, his mountain-climbing dog from Kenogami, a German shepherd given to him by Sir William Price, the president of the Price Brothers lumbering consortium. Many a night they would bed down on spruce boughs when the "Chief" was exploring virgin country and cutting trails north of Shawbridge to Ste-Agathe.

On January 31, 1930, Herman Smith Johannsen became a Canadian citizen. He had always felt more at home in Canada than in the United States: "Here we have two languages, the pace is more relaxed and the Laurentians seem so much like the land of my birth." For the next sixty-five years many of his skiing outings would originate at the Shawbridge Club, which he had joined in 1928, and to which he would impart something of his own spirit. As George Jost, a renowned skier himself, put it, "... we learned from our respected elder the beauty and serenity of the deep woods, the sleeping frozen landscape, and the real brotherhood of friendship."

Late in the fall of 1931 (just two years before Hitler became Germany's chancellor) "Jackrabbit" made another decision that was to affect Laurentian skiing and the Shawbridge Club as well. After the Crash and the onset of the Depression, his business pretty well petered out in Montreal and by this time his three children, Alice, Peggy, and Bob were moving along in school. Herman and his wife, Alice, decided to move to the Laurentians. The manager at the Shawbridge Club, Leigh Harding, helped them look for a place. For a while they moved in with one of Harding's relatives, then to a small house near the C.P.R. station, and in the fall of 1933 to a cottage in Val-Morin.

As the Depression deepened, it is not surprising that "Jackrabbit" turned to what he knew best, skiing, and if he could make a livelihood from it – instructing, cutting trails, guiding – so much the better. The pickings were skimpy and sometimes Alice and the children did not know where their next meal was coming from. The way it all turned out in the end, would they have wanted to change the script written by the "Chief"? His philosophy was simple: "You have good weather and you have bad weather, but for those who wait long enough the sun always comes out again."

F.M. Van Wagner with his wife, Catherine, c. 1938

From 1920, "Van" was a professor of Phys. Ed. at McGill and mentor to the McGill Outing Club. He skied several thousand miles in the Laurentians (counting every one), cut and cared for several trails, and often invited his good friend, "Jackrabbit", to his Camp Nominingue, founded to connect young people with outdoor living.

(Peter Van Wagner Collection)

There was no lack of requests for his services. The parish priest, at what later was called Mont-Tremblant village, fought as hard against depressed conditions in the upper Laurentians as Curé Labelle had fought to encourage tourism. Father Charles-Hector Deslauriers, whose reserved exterior concealed a man of action, had noticed the enthusiasm of the children at the ski meets "Jackrabbit" was organizing for them so he asked him to help lay out a ski trail and a jump at Tremblant.

Two days after receiving this request, Johannsen skied forty miles to the village. Father Deslaurier describes the result:

"The ski jump and trail became village projects ... every weekend was a fiesta. The village got its laughter and confidence back and was able to organize and start other community projects. Chief Jackrabbit Johannsen had demonstrated how a village could be self-organizing. It was like a miracle."

Already "Jackrabbit" sensed that the Laurentians could become a prime tourist attraction bringing jobs and money to a region of high unemployment. So he set about cutting and co-ordinating trails, the result being the famous Maple Leaf trail looping some sixty-five miles from Shawbridge in the south to Labelle (named after the great colonizer) in the north. For his outstanding contribution to the area the highest peak in the Laurentians (3,150 feet) would be named Johannsen.

In the Thirties the favourite trails at the Shawbridge Club were also acquiring their own names, often as a result of some curious incident. The "Fallen Women" always intrigued members of both sexes; "The Madonna" which I often skied, was marked by a weather-worn statue of the Virgin standing precariously on an old stump behind a wire fence; "Flypaper Hills" had something to do with climbing over-hanging snow drifts; "A Flight's Delight" was often misconstrued, much to the annoyance of the veterans, because the name referred to an Air Force flight-wing; the "Barking Dog" is self-explanatory and some of us have the scars to prove it; (I was there with a group from the Club one sunny winter's morning when the owner came out wielding a shot gun to warn us off); "The Water Fall", "The Patriarch", and "The Tracks" are more contemporary and "The Chief's", down a gully at the end of the golf course, a stream running through it and bright red cardinals singing in the spring sunshine, was a lovely retreat named for the Shawbridge Club's premier skier.

Jean and Drummond Ross (Joan Ross Clark Collection)

All these trails were well-travelled despite the hardships caused by the Depression which affected the members of the Shawbridge Club, as it did everyone else. The Johannsens sold their Winton Six for a Studebaker, then sold the Studebaker, at the same time dispensing with their daily newspaper and spending no money on non-essentials. A Club member, George McTaggart, joined his friend, Drummond Ross (both having lost their jobs) to create a map-making business. Ross's daughter, Joan Ross Clark remembers:

"In the summer, we'd go up to the Laurentians in an old Ford car with a rumbleseat. When the canvas top wore out, Mother made another one on her sewing machine. We'd stop and Dad would go rushing off into the bush. He had learned map-making at the Royal Military College in Kingston before he went overseas with the Royal Horse Guards Artillery." George's wife, Lois Ibbotson, also recalls the map-making venture. "It saved their lives for those couple of years between 1932 and 1935 when they were without a regular job. I spent quite a lot of time making cases for the maps out of very thin leather." A large Ross-McTaggart map still graces the walls of the Shawbridge Club, especially useful for marathon Saturday morning skiers who return late for lunch and want to figure out where they got lost.

Other members of the Club also felt the pinch. Margaret Watt, whose parents the Allan Turner Bones, joined the Club in 1930, at first did not go up to Shawbridge with them: "In the earlier days of the Depression we children didn't go to the Club. There was no money. My Dad was in construction and nothing was being built. I was the eldest and I was pulled out of private school."

Alice Johannsen, Herman's eldest child, remembers the breadlines she saw "every day on my way to school as the streetcar made its way along Ste-Catherine street, where block-long double lines of desperate men shivered in the cold as they waited their turn for a free bowl of hot soup and a crust of bread at an emergency shelter."

Ann Foster, sister of Alex, with her husband, Wilson Mellen, and daughter, Beverly, 1939 (Beverly Mellen Sofin Collection)

Mabel Selby Bryson remembers how people rallied round in the Depression and helped each other. She arrived back in Shawbridge with twenty dollars in her pocket and two children to raise. Mr. Harding gave her a job:

"Shawbridge was a very friendly place; everybody knew each other. French and English went to each other's weddings and church socials. In the summer I worked for some of the Jewish families. The synagogue was right there by the bridge. Someone gave me a tent and I camped as close to the river as I could with my two boys in the summer. In the winter I rented accommodations and I walked to work at the Club except when it was too stormy when Mr. Harding would come for me. One night, one of the women members handed me an envelope: 'This is for a summer holiday for you and your boys.' I nearly keeled over. We spent two weeks at a friend's cabin, a holiday my boys never forgot."

For some the Club was a refuge from the oppressive social and economic conditions. The fees were modest and the living was much more affordable than that charged by the inns then dotting the Laurentians. "Many families had been devastated by the Depression, mine among them," explains Bruce Kippen, "but all that was left behind at the Club."

After arriving by train Friday and after a good night's sleep, activities began early Saturday morning with bells and bustle. Priscilla Penfield Chester recalls that she and her sister, Mary, were "awakened by a knock at the door and Walter coming in with a tea tray and setting it down so he could close our windows, then asking, 'Cream or sugar?' Then Mr. Birks and my father (Wilder Penfield) would bring breakfast to their wives." Diana Drew Togneri recalls "reaching for the glass of water beside my bed to find I was drinking a thin layer of ice." No wonder. "The thermometer on the post outside the front door one Saturday morning," writes George Currie, "according to Senator Hugessen read minus 40 degrees F."

"All out!" for Peggy and Peter John ("P.J.") Austin, aged four months
(Peggy Johannsen Austin Collection)

Those going down to a sunny dining room for breakfast sometimes had to cope with stronger aromas than the ones coming from Harry Lawton's delicious bread. Sue Birks Dwyer and her mother can't forget the kippers. "We sat as far from them as possible because of the dreadful smell." Sometimes after a late party on Friday night, there would be an 'accident' at breakfast, salt in the sugar bowl, or, as Herbie Lewis recalls, "Boydie Welsford serving John Trim a bowl of warm milk with a sardine floating in it."

Often too, the early breakfasters finished their main course (thick porridge, bacon and eggs, pancakes or French toast drenched in Quebec maple syrup and the infamous kippers) and went on to their second cup of coffee while comparing notes on which ski wax to use. Then they would hear a clatter in the hallway, lined with boots and clothes, and this wiry man in his thick grey sweater with his weather-beaten face, eyes as blue as a glacial lake, would burst into the dining room and yell, "Who's for skiing this morning? All out!"

Priscilla Penfield remembers: "At breakfast, Mr. Johannsen would come over from his house in the village, lean over us, arms across our shoulders, and exclaim, 'Eat lots of porridge, you'll need it if you want to be trail snails and come out in the woods with me. Who's coming?'"

There was always a group of younger people in the main hall, often rubbing their skis and inhaling the pungent fumes of the pine tar from the ski shop downstairs while they waited for Mr. Johannsen to give them their marching orders. Orian Stewart Hodgson didn't much fancy cross-country skiing but "in order to be allowed to ski on the Big Hill in the afternoon you had to go for miles in the morning with Mr. Johannsen setting a wicked pace." Virginia Birks Alexandor says "Jackrabbit" eventually worked them up "to a trip that was seventeen miles long, then helped us build a fire for lunch to heat our tea and cook little cubes of meat on long sticks."

Warm clothing was necessary. "I wore thick wool riding breeks," writes Charlotte Millen, "and a Grenfell parka belted with a colourful ceinture fléchée and a pair of boy's laced boots that were buckled onto my oh-so-long heavy skis. My boot tops were wound around with woven wool puttees, ostensibly to keep the snow from getting inside my boots."

Sometimes the morning skiing took a different form. Several members of the Club underwrote the cost of hiring a professional ski instructor and in 1937 Mario Gabriel came out from Switzerland. Diana Togneri says she and other children "would trek over to the bottom of the Big Hill to be drilled by Mario, always so sleek and suntanned with the inevitable dark glasses and all greased up to get a tan." Mario was a hard taskmaster and a bit of a martinet. "Mario kept us doing endless snowplow turns on the practice hill," Diana continues, "until we were able to do a Christiana turn." To Priscilla Penfield, Mario was "the charming, small, but so handsome ski instructor from Switzerland. Lucky for him he had a wife as we fell in love with him and his delightful enthusiasm and ability to treat us as equals. He made it all fun."

Boyd and Charlotte Millen c. 1935. (Charlotte Millen Collection)

John Trim recalls a moment when Mario's instruction made a big difference:

"My strongest memory of the Club comes when I was about six years old, 1937 it would be. My parents and I set out on the train from Shawbridge to St-Sauveur. It was a lovely spring day when we left. After we got off the train, it began to cloud over, and by the time we crossed over the mountain ridge to get to the Big Hill, the weather became horrible with hard blowing snow. We picked up a bunch of stragglers, some who had been hiding under trees from the storm.

"I was deathly afraid of coming down the Big Hill, but somehow I managed to snowplough and made it down to the bottom. Mario's lessons, which I had barely learned, made all the difference that time."

Mario Gabriel with Dody Russel Williams. (Frances Williams Collection)

Mario's instruction was also an important factor in the Test Runs. These were held for the younger members on a course near the Big Hill that involved a hairpin turn through the Devil's Throat. Anne Henry Murdoch describes how much was at stake:

"This was serious business because there were real stopwatches used. The fortunate participants won a Shawbridge Laurentian Lodge Club badge with one, two or three golden maple leaves on it, depending on the level achieved. Once a year, there was a race held for the school children of the village with a wondrous display of prizes, everything from skis, to bindings and goggles ..."

Mary Anne Miller writes about "endlessly side-stepping up the racing hill, packing it carefully, and then flying down hanging on with all ten toes to get my badge." The Shawbridge Club started them early in those days. Jane Russel and her husband, "remember our daughter, Ginny, three years old, skiing down between Daddy's skis, winning a prize and being congratulated at the bottom of the hill by 'Chief' Johannsen." Inevitably there would be an accident. Banty Reid was there "when Herb Murphy crashed near the Devil's Throat and broke a bone in his spine in the neck area. He had to be handled carefully but managed to get back to the Club and down to the hospital where he recovered nicely."

Sometimes, all this could be quite terrifying for a child. Anne Hale Wonham, daughter of "Povey" Hale, remembers the ski instructor with trepidation:

"Mario, the ski pro, was fierce, scary, and a disciplinarian who had us quaking in our boots. We had to pack that ski hill up and down before we were allowed on it. I remember one absolutely terrifying run down to qualify for my two maple leaves. I never did get three. Dody Williams, whom we all liked, said, 'This isn't going to work,' and very quietly she took us kids out in the afternoon. Suddenly, skiing was fun again."

The Duchess of Leuchtenberg with Napoleonic memorabilia. (Photo Michael Drummond)

A few Club members had also had a lesson or two from no less a personage than the Duke Dimitri de Leuchtenberg, a fine European ski instructor, brought out in 1933 by the Montreal Ski Club. The Duke was a twice-wounded Russian Cavalry officer and a descendant of Napoleon's Empress, Josephine. His wife, Katia, had been married to a White Russian in the court of Czar Nicholas. During the Revolution he was executed and Katia, too, narrowly escaped death from a firing squad. She helped her second husband with his ski school in St-Sauveur and she lived to attend the sixtieth anniversary party of the Shawbridge Club.

Anne Hale Wonham recalls that "there was an extraordinary bond among all these people. There was a sense when you went into that living room – which seemed vast to me – of inter-generational tolerance. The kids would be playing close to the adults. It was a warm kind of community that was comfortable for a child. Dody Russel Williams was part of the older group, an extraordinary woman, with a braid wound tight around her head and piercing blue eyes that looked right through you. She had this wonderful capacity to focus on you as though you were the only person in the world. She was wonderful with young people; she treated them like adults and could immediately sense who needed encouragement."

After the travails and triumphs of a day on the slopes there was a special treat which Priscilla Penfield vividly describes:

"How we loved High Tea! We piled into the big living room joining the family groups. The trays for each group, relaxing and chatting in deep old easy-chairs and sofas, were generously laden with warm buttered scones and jam and huge pots of tea. Then, we would settle down to silly games of cards like 'Cheat!', or checkers or try our luck at the pool table across the hall or ping-pong in the room at the right of the entrance."

Then there was the famous Bottle Race: "It was run," writes Frances McLeod Hamilton, "in the spring when the melting snow filled the creek at the edge of the property. Empty bottles – Scotch, Gin, whatever – were given the name of the participant and thrown in the stream high up, then followed down by the owners. Each of the bottles represented a horse and bets were placed for the winner. I was about fourteen at the time so I think Dad took care of my bets. It was a great event, and a sure sign of spring." Just in case their bottle became stuck, many racers took along a pole to help it along.

The Bottle Race - Bottles and poles at the ready
From (left to right): Bill Yuile, Kirk and Fran McLeod, Eddie Renouf. Second row: Helen Renouf, Dody Russel Williams. Third row center: "Povey" Forbes Hale. (Frances Williams Collection)

One icy weekend Bruce Russel remembers, "it was too dangerous to ski, so a group of us got together and played broomball on the golf course on the ice and had a super time." Nor was this sort of activity beneath the parents despite incredulous stares by the villagers. John Trim says that "one warm spring day, they headed out to the golf course and had a great time playing snow golf on their skis beating a black golf ball around in the general direction of the holes. Nobody really knew where the holes were but that made no difference. This sort of thing usually happened only after the pre-lunch drinks."

More experienced skiers would take longer trips even in difficult weather. Lindsay Jarrett recalls "taking the train up the line to St-Sauveur or Ste-Marguerite and skiing back picnicking on the way, and building a fire in the snow and cooking cubes of steak over it. There was ski-joring and sleigh rides on cold frosty moonlit nights and games, story-telling and sing-songs around a cozy fire in the Club."

And sometimes there were late night sports, as Senator Landon Pearson recalls. (The Senator's parents, Hugh and Alice Mackenzie, joined the Club in the later Thirties.)

Jeff and Wilder Penfield, Jr. on the Big Hill.

(Priscilla Penfield Chester Collection)

"I don't remember the physical structure of the Club very well although later on, as my palate matured, I really appreciated the food which was remarkably good. However, I am embarrassed to remember my first foray into 'necking' which took place in the lounge after the gang had gone out to some coffee-shop in the village. Of course, I am sure the boy, whoever he was, would have equal difficulty remembering me! Still, those were innocent times."

So did the Shawbridge Club offer its members a respite from the stresses and strains of the dirty Thirties.

First Shawbridge Club group at the White Peak Cabin on top of Tremblant, March, 1935. Left to right: Donnie Cleghorn, founding member of the Shawbridge Club; Gordon Hanson, also a founding member; Mac Yuile, first president; "Hugie" Hugessen, later a Senator; Kay Terroux; Forbes Hale; Ferdie Terroux; August Burmeister (cook); Vero Wynne-Edwards; Arthur Terroux; Willie Legaré (guide); unidentified; "Jackrabbit"; seated, Lindsay Hall. Photo by Fred Taylor. (Peggy Johannsen Austin Collection)

THE WHITE PEAK CABIN

Although he had yet to ski on the mountain peak that was to honour his name, Herman Johannsen had been exploring the Devil's River region of Mont-Tremblant park on skis as early as 1925, about the time he first began dropping in to the Shawbridge Club.

There is some confusion about who first climbed Tremblant (3,150 feet), the most famous mountain in the Laurentians. Perhaps it was the native hunters of long ago. There was activity around the mountain as early as 1902 when a healthcare giver named Elizabeth Ward set up a fishing camp at the foot of Tremblant to help her patients recover from tuberculosis after they had spent some time in the sanitoria at Ste-Agathe.

In her memoir, *The Awakening of the Laurentians,* Frances Wheeler claims her father, George, was the first to climb Mont-Tremblant in 1907 when he planted a Union Jack on its highest peak. George Wheeler was an athletic man, dapper and vigorous, his personality reflecting the charms and proprieties of the old school. From his home at Chazy on the shores of Lake Champlain in upstate New York, he heard about the lumbering fortunes being made in Northern Quebec. So in 1893, he bought a stretch of virgin pine forest near St-Jovite, moved there with his wife, Lucille Aldridge, built a home on the shores of Lac-Seraphin (the native word for "peaceful waters", later changed to Lac-Ouimet after the local priest named it for himself), and started a sawmill.

Three years later, the Wheelers' house burned down, so they lived in the boathouse while George built a new home on a rock promontory called Gray Rocks, between the lake and the mountains. Having decided to get out of the lumber business (the sawmill had also burned), the Wheelers planned to turn their new home into a ten-room inn that was to become Gray Rocks, the first year-round Laurentian resort.

After a forest fire ravaged Mont-Tremblant during the summer of 1908, a fire tower was erected on its peak with a path leading up from Lac-Tremblant. George Wheeler's sons, Tom and Harry, used this path to climb to the top on skis in 1916. In 1927, Tom was one of the first (after Émile Cochand) to open a ski school in the Laurentians but, at this early stage, there does not seem to have been much skiing on Tremblant itself. Tom was also busy developing what became the oldest commercial airline in the country. He had learned to fly at Princeton and later his father bought him a Curtis Seagull aircraft used for fire patrol and hunting trips.

It was during this period that McGill University's Red Birds Ski Club was founded by three young men in 1928. One of the trio was Harry Pangman, a premier Canadian skier, and later a member of the Shawbridge Club. (The McGill Daily, reporting on this event incorrectly, called it the Red Wing Ski Club.) Many of the Red Birds, hot-doggers and free-wheelers, became champion skiers. (Harry Pangman was a Canadian Olympian in 1932.) They developed new techniques, which resulted in downhill skiing being recognized as a separate discipline in world competition.

One of the Red Birds' founders, Harry Pangman, racing in the Kandahar, 1935. (Jill Pangman Collection)

In 1929, coming back on the train from a McGill-Dartmouth ski meet, organized by the Red Birds, Herman Johannsen was made an honorary member of the Red Birds, called by Bill Ball in *I Skied the Thirties*, "the most exclusive ski club in Canada." This exclusivity went hand in hand with a fierce competitive spirit. One of the locales the Red Birds used near their clubhouse at St-Sauveur was "Hill 70", named after a Canadian battle victory in France with troops led by Sir Arthur Currie, principal of McGill. At one of their field days on "Hill 70" the competition was so keen, and the team's supporters so enthusiastic, that "both sides of the main hill were lined with members of the McGill Officers' Training Corps, armed with rifles to keep the crowd in place."

It is not surprising then that on April 13, 1930, the first official expedition up Mont-Tremblant for the purpose of skiing was organized and led by Red Birds, including Harry Pangman and "Jackrabbit" and his dog Caesar (the dog, Ken, had been killed in 1926). Harry Pangman writes about the trip in *Jackrabbit, His First Hundred Years*, a splendid encomium to Herman, edited by Brian Powell:

First skiing ascent of Mont Tremblant, 1930. (Left to right): Stirling Maxwell, Neil Stewart, Harry Pangman and "Jackrabbit"

Harry Pangman to Catharine McKenty in front of the fireplace at the Shawbridge Club: "On an early Red Bird trip up Tremblant, we woke up at four in the morning to find ourselves in the midst of a howling snow storm. 'Jackrabbit' got us young guys down the mountain safely, swinging from the tops of spruce trees."

(Photo Frederick Taylor from the Betty Kemp Maxwell Collection)

"Certainly it was Herman who first introduced us to Mont-Tremblant. The train up on Saturday, the night at Wheelers' or Pinoteau's, and up the mountain the next day. One skied from the station or inn, to and up the mountain, and lunched on top, followed by the bushwhacking run down through the powder snow, and the ski back to the station."

It was then that Harry Pangman formed his first impression of "Jackrabbit's" uncanny ability:

"Bursting out of the upper slopes into a small clearing, he suddenly found himself straddling the fire-ranger's telephone line which had suddenly come out from under the snow. As if this were a normal occurrence, he rode it for some 20 feet getting higher and higher above the ground, until finally, losing momentum, he flipped off, dropped some ten feet to the ground, landed on his feet, and continued on down the hill, albeit a bit bow-legged."

Later Jackrabbit led a small group of Red Birds for a week's trek through Tremblant Park and further north, sleeping and eating in the frigid Canadian winter. Lean and abstemious, Herman was in charge of the food supplies. What George Jost remembers is how the group had to improvise to keep enough food on the table:

" ... our Friday evening meal consisted of fresh bread we had picked up at a lumber camp the previous day, and two partridges which a trapper had given us in exchange for two of the loaves of bread. We roasted the two birds on a spit in the trapper's open fireplace and bunked that night in his primitive log cabin."

Three members of the Shawbridge Club, Herman, Percy Douglas and Harry Pangman organized the first Quebec Kandahar race in 1932. The name Kandahar comes from a town in Afghanistan where, in 1832, a siege was relieved by a British force led by Field Marshall Frederick Sleigh Roberts (later Lord Roberts of Kandahar), who was himself a keen skier. Peter Gillespie, one of the contestants, gives this vivid description of the first Quebec Kandahar:

"The starting post was in the clearing just under the fire tower, and ... one by one ... the frozen racers disappeared into the thick trees below. They looked as if they were falling down a grain elevator shaft. Every now and then floated up the sounds of a rattling crash, followed by faint curses ... About half-way down the top part, I passed someone with his feet in a tree and his head hanging down the hill. He had given up the unequal struggle and was resting quietly ...

"Further down everyone began to pile up and I passed two people wrestling together in a heap of rocks. Someone in front of me fell down and I ran over him, then he got up and ran over me. By this time there were bits of equipment strewn all over the place, mitts and caps, broken ski poles and pieces of skis ... One by one the others came in. Nearly everyone had a bruise somewhere; but they all agreed it had been a wonderful race, and that they had enjoyed every minute of it – now that it was over."

Harry Pangman, 1934 (Jill Pangman Collection)

Harry Pangman, a sturdy athlete with powerful shoulders and legs and a strong ruddy face, won the downhill portion of the first Quebec Kandahar, pole-riding most of the way, in fifteen minutes and ten seconds. (George Jost's joint times in the downhill and slalom made him the overall winner.)

In March, 1935, a group of strong skiers at the Shawbridge Club decided to have their own go at Tremblant, the trembling mountain that the native peoples more than a thousand years before had given the name "Manitou Ewitchi", the mountain of the dreaded spirits.

The group, fourteen in all under the leadership of the "Chief", was an interesting mix. There was "Mac" Yuile, the Club's first president, a quiet man with a subdued way of speaking but a natural leader; Vero Wynne-Edwards, a professor in the Zoology department at McGill would gain international recognition for his work on the evolution of birds and animals; Mostyn Lewis, an insurance broker, had distinguished himself in the Royal Flying Corps during World War One; Don Cleghorn, one of the founders of the Club, would become a curator at the Redpath Museum and an artist in his own right; "Hugie" Hugessen, a distinguished Montreal lawyer who had served overseas with the McGill battery of the Canadian Heavy Artillery, was the only Etonian ever appointed to the Canadian Senate; Lindsay Hall, highly decorated in the war was a shy retiring

Montreal bachelor; Gordon Hanson was a veteran and a member of one of Montreal's leading investment and banking firms, and soon to be president of the Shawbridge Club.

And there was Forbes "Povey" Hale, a personnel officer with Dominion Engineering who had a remarkable war, guarding an open ammunition dump on the beaches at Gallipoli, leading his men to safety by starlight in the Egyptian desert, an outdoorsman and strong skier with a sense of humour and panache that endeared him to his men and to his fellow members at the Club; Kay Terroux, the only woman on the trip and the wife of Ferdie, was one of the early women to earn a doctorate at McGill; and the Terroux brothers, Arthur, a Montreal lawyer and friend of the Johannsen and Harding children and Ferdie, a physics professor at McGill, rounded out the group. The Terroux were a well-known French-Canadian family; their father imported whiskey and other spirits from overseas and the family mixed easily in both cultures.

Fred Taylor, who took the photograph of the group in front of the Whitepeak Cabin, built by the Wheelers on the mountain, was the brother of the industrial tycoon, Edward Plunkett Taylor.He was an able artist of the Laurentians, a skier and boxer and while at McGill studying architecture, lived in the student ghetto with a left-wing group that included Frank Scott.

Ferdie Terroux, in a letter to fellow Club member and skier, Jane Yuile Lewis, has left us the only written story of this memorable ascent up the mountain, which he titles 'A 1935 Adventure':

"Dearly beloved Jane:

In spite of the fact that past the age of 80 years, my memory of names has suffered greatly, I will try to give you some information about 1935.

The whole story concerns a very wonderful ski party on the top of Tremblant. The party was organized by my brother, Arthur Terroux, perhaps helped by his close friend, Lindsay [Hall]. The entire show was made possible by the close collaboration of the two brothers Wheeler who presided over Gray Rocks Inn at St-Jovite. The brothers organized every local detail. They owned the single log cabin that sat on the very top of Tremblant and three of their staff carried enormous supplies of all sorts – food, fuel, blankets which fed (sic) the whole party and helped in every way.

Sleighs from Gray Rocks delivered the whole group at the foot of the mountain on Friday evening. Each member of the party carried all his clothes and kit in his own packsack, and climbed to the top of the mountain in the moonlight along an ancient trail made by the fire ranger. It was a long climb that some members found somewhat fatiguing.

Two days were spent on the mountain, and the whole group skied along the summit ridge on Saturday. On Sunday, the entire group made their way down the Kandahar ski track which was in very difficult condition. Back to Gray Rocks and returned by train to Montreal.

Ferdie Terroux"

Tic, toc, wind up the clock, and let's start the weekend over again
February, Friday the thirteenth! until Sunday night N.E.D. 1925

The eager skiers gather, sharp at ten.(?)
Colours adorn the women; looks, the men (?) H.O. M.G. L.D.
No more do skirts the active female vex,
For breeches grace the limbs of either sex.
Soon they are off across the barren hills,
And merry laughter speaks of frequent spills.
But little heed they pay to Newton's laws
Though every tumble finds therein its cause,
For all the winds are keen, and swift each run,
And men and mountains glory in the sun.
Then home at last they turn, at quickened pace
To eat — with more of appetite than grace.

F.R.S.

Unpublished lines by Frank R. Scott, poet, legal scholar, and teacher. In Huntly Drummond's guest book, "Wild Thyme Cottage", 1925.
(Bruce McNiven Collection)

THE GOLDEN SKIER

Joe and Mary Ryan (Photo John O'Rear)

Almost ten years after the Shawbridge Club made the pages of *The New Yorker*, another American appeared on the scene in 1938. His name was Joe Ryan, a wealthy, upper-crust Philadelphian of Irish background who spoke French, was called "the golden skier" and, as Louise Arbique recounts in *Tremblant: Following the Dream*, would leave his imprint on the Laurentians forever.

Born in 1906, Joseph Bondurand Ryan was a grandson of Thomas Fortune Ryan, a powerful tycoon who made his money through railways and street cars, not to mention sharp business practices, bribery and general skullduggery. Joe's father, William, a mining engineer, left his family well off. He died when his son was two months old.

Perhaps because of his father's mining background, Joe wanted to explore the wilderness. As a boy, he vacationed with his family in New Brunswick and, in 1923, when only seventeen, took off from home and ended up as a driller in Rouyn-Noranda shortly after the rich Noranda gold, copper and silver mines were discovered. (It was during these years that he became fluent in French.) The next summer, Joe bulked up his muscles swinging sledge hammers for the Hammond gold mine in Alaska.

He returned to Philadelphia to sell insurance at which – a born salesman – he excelled. When his grandfather died in 1928, leaving a fortune estimated at $142 million, Joe inherited $125,000, an enormous sum in those days. He bought a seat on the Philadelphia Stock Exchange, a venture on which he lost money when the markets crashed in 1929.

Although he had married in 1930, Joe realized he didn't want to be stuck in cities; he was an outdoors man with something of his grandfather's pioneering drive. Explaining to his wife and children (he would soon have three) that he wanted to explore a business deal, he headed north to Chibougamau looking for mineral deposits. He came up empty but that did nothing to satiate his wanderlust and spirit of adventure.

After divorcing his wife in 1936 when he was thirty, Ryan hooked up with his cousin Theodore, an excellent skier, to tour the best ski resorts in Europe. One evening, Joe, a betting man, ran into a famous jockey named Sid Hirst. They not only wagered on a horse race in Australia but decided to fly out there to see the action. But instead of taking the plane to

Australia, they hopped on one to Austria. Perhaps they slurred their words and the ticket agent misunderstood.

Nothing daunted, they skied all over Europe where the idea of building a ski resort of his own some day likely popped into Ryan's head. Finally, the two intrepid skiers headed for Rome where they met the Maharajah of Jaipur, and India where they hunted tigers and bunked with another prince in his palace. On their way home, they broke their journey at Bangkok, managing to fight off a cholera epidemic with copious quantities of brandy and champagne.

When Joe Ryan returned to Philadelphia, the executor of his grandfather's estate, Bernard Baruch, a respected economic advisor to several American presidents, told him he was sick and tired of Joe's asking for advances on his income and urged him to stop living it up, get a decent job and settle down.

With his head still full of those magnificent ski spreads in Europe, Joe's response was to visit the resort in Sun Valley, Idaho, then in January, 1938, he arranged a skiing trip in New England where, unfortunately, he found little snow. That's why he happened to fetch up at Gray Rocks, the Wheelers' place on Lac-Ouimet. There he met the celebrated American journalist, Lowell Thomas, himself an outdoors man who, like Ryan, had skied extensively throughout Europe.

Joe Ryan's Mountain (Photo Jan Brunner)

Thomas had arranged for Tom Wheeler to fly a small group to the foot of Mont-Tremblant and for his brother, Harry, to lead them on skis to the top. Overhearing Lowell Thomas and the Wheelers discussing the trip in the dining room, Joe Ryan came over to their table and asked if he could come along. They agreed, so on a clear cold day, (ten degrees below zero F.), they flew to the base of the mountain, then made the arduous climb of several hours using seal-skins under their skis for a better grip.

When they reached the top, Joe Ryan was stunned. In bright sunshine he looked out from "Manitou Ewitchi" and saw what the first hunters had seen so long ago, a rolling landscape of snowy mountains and frozen lakes glittering like silver watches in the light.

Joe's mind, as clear as the view, began to race. He thought of the splendid resorts he had seen in Europe. He thought of the war, now looming on the horizon, that would cut off skiing in the Alps. And right here in this breathtaking place, he could already see the ski resort of his dreams. There was only one problem. It was too difficult to climb the mountain. Joe Ryan turned to his companions and vowed, "I'll fix that." And he did.

It was not long before skiers at the Shawbridge Club were looking at Tremblant with renewed interest. George Currie describes an early trip to the mountain organized by Mr. Johannsen:

"I think we were a group of six or seven boys, all aged about fourteen to sixteen. We went by train to Tremblant, then by sleigh to the single chairlift on the south side. In the gathering dusk, it must have been 3:30 in the afternoon or later, we went up the mountain by chair and T-bar to the top [1939]. Jackrabbit then led us through the woods to the north side, completely undeveloped in those days. He located a small log cabin with its chimney pipe sticking up through the snow. Using our skis as shovels, we dug down and opened the door.

"Inside were log bunks on each side and a pot-bellied stove in the middle. We spent the night there with Jackrabbit sleeping on the hard logs next to the stove which he kept stoked all night to keep us warm. The next morning Jackrabbit led us on our downhill skis across hill and dale to Johannsen Peak. From there he struck off on a downhill diagonal track while we tried to keep up with him. We emerged precisely at the bottom of the Nansen Run on the south side exactly as he intended. Utterly exhausted, we slept most of the way back to the Shawbridge Club on the train. It was only much later that I realized Mr. Johannsen was probably then well into his sixties."

"Jackrabbit" on top of Tremblant with Nicki and Wheeler dog c. 1930 (Peggy Johannsen Austin Collection)

Other members enjoyed the skiing closer to home, especially in the spring when the warmer days of March and April brought their own rewards, like sunning on the Big Hill with aluminum reflectors and, as Diana Togneri recalls, "skiing without jackets, drinks outside on the side balcony at noon watching the ice-cream being hand-cranked for Sunday lunch, just by the kitchen door."

There was also the Ice Palace. Frances and Russ Williams remember the staff making an ice palace outside on the front lawn. "They moved in wooden summer chairs and we sat there in the spring with a drink before lunch after a morning of skiing." They also recall the little skating rink in front of the Club. "I remember Natalie Harding and her brother, John, figure skating on that little rink under the evergreens."

Occasionally, there was excitement at the sight of a sporty car, still a novelty up north. Jane Russel remembers her brother, Bruce, "and Tom King arriving back at the Club in Tom's convertible after spring skiing at Mont-Gabriel – roof down, shirt sleeves rolled up and sporting a terrific tan."

On the afternoon of December 11, 1936, before they gathered in the lounge for pre-dinner drinks, the members crowded around the Marconi radio to hear Edward VIII announce his abdication because he could not reign "without the woman I love." And less than two years later, on September 30, 1938, they listened to the British Prime Minister, Neville Chamberlain, on his return from his discussions with Herr Hitler at Munich, announce that he had brought "peace in our time".

Walter serving drinks in the spring sunshine. Major Clyde Drew (l.) with his wife Beatrice and Terry Terroux, March 17, 1932.
(Diana Drew Togneri Collection)

"I used to love to go to Dad's warehouse off the Mountain Street bridge, just across the road from Rockhead's Paradise, with all the aromas, cookies from England, whiskey from Scotland, shellac from India and those dark cherry pound cakes at Christmas, all mixed in with the smells of paint and varnish." **Diana Drew Togneri**

THE END OF AN ERA

By the time Joe Ryan climbed Mont-Tremblant for the first time, the style of skiing, much affected by the proliferation of rope tows, was changing rapidly. Until the mid-Thirties downhill, cross-country, competition and ski jumping were all simply known as skiing and one type of ski was used for every style.

Shops in Montreal like Arlington Cycle and Sports were now advertising metal poles to replace bamboo, improved edges and dual purpose bindings with adjustable settings, one for cross-country, the other for downhill. No one took advantage of these changes more than the Red Birds Ski Club which had a chalet near the bottom of the Big Hill in St-Sauveur. The Red Birds were dare-devil skiers who began to develop new techniques for roaring down a mountain, poles over their heads, stopping any way they could, even if it meant flinging themselves to the ground. With founding members like Harry Pangman, the Red Birds pushed the envelope of championship Canadian skiing.

Not to be outdone, a group of keen women skiers founded the Penguin Ski Club in 1932, the first women's ski club in Canada. From an attractive clubhouse built for them in St-Sauveur by John Molson, the Penguins developed some of the country's great skiers, the Paré and Wurtele sisters, Peggy and Alice Johannsen, and the Kemps, Barbara and Betty. Some later became members of the Shawbridge Club. In fact, the founding of the Penguins may well have influenced the Shawbridge Club to accept its first lady members. Hitherto it had been a male bastion to which the gentlemen skiers could bring their wives or other ladies as guests. In 1936 after the death of her husband, Mrs. Lawrence Kelly became the first honorary female member.

Ken Farmer, "Le Clou", steaming to the 1936 Olympics (Ken Farmer Collection)

Someone who frequently brought his wife, Lorrayne, initially to the Laurentians and later to the Shawbridge Club, was Ken Farmer. "It was when I first met my wife in the Thirties at McGill that I took up cross-country skiing; she was very keen and we went up north every weekend."

Ken Farmer was not only an enthusiastic cross-country skier. He was a pivotal member of McGill's

"Red Raiders" hockey team, which won three league titles in the 1933-34 season, helped by the awesome power play led by the "Four Horsemen", one of whom was Kenny Farmer. In 1936 while he was playing for the Montreal Victorias, Farmer was invited to join Canada's Olympic hockey team. At the winter games in the German Alps near Munich, Kenny had a memorable experience:

"The game was to be played outdoors on a regulation rink with artificial ice. It was a beautiful day with blue skies. The ice was beginning to melt so a colleague and I were sent out to inspect to see whether or not the game should be postponed.

"As we climbed back over the boards and headed down an outdoors passageway – between the boards and the stands of hidden spectators – we noticed a commotion among the spectators. They had all risen and were shouting Heil Hitler.

"A moment later as we continued down the outdoor passageway towards our dressing room, whom did we run into but Hitler himself surrounded by his retinue. The Führer looked startled, then raised his arm in salute and barked "Heil Hitler" in German. After a moment's hesitation I thought, "What the heck!" and returned the unexpected greeting with my own "Heil Hitler". The German leader remained for at least part of the game. In the end we won the silver medal for hockey."

After news of Hitler's aggression against Czechoslovakia and the futility of Chamberlain's peace mission, members of the Shawbridge Club, like many other Canadians, feared the outbreak of another world war. It was perhaps ironic that the president of the Club in that fateful year, 1939, was a General in the Canadian army.

Major-General Edouard de Bellefeuille Panet, President of the Shawbridge Club, 1939
(Elizabeth Fairbairn Collection)

Brigadier-General Edouard de Bellefeuille Panet, C.M.G., D.S.O., was a much-decorated veteran of World War One who had accompanied the First Canadian Division to France in 1915. Among other distinctions he was awarded the Legion d'Honneur, Croix de Chevalier for "gallant and distinguished service in the field" by the President of the French Republic. After the war, General Panet became the head of the Investigation Department of the Canadian Pacific Railway and an accomplished skier into the bargain. He joined the Shawbridge Club in the late Twenties. An army document describes General Panet as "intelligent, alert, tall [just over six feet] and well built." Bruce Kippen remembers the General as "tall and handsome with a military bearing but very approachable especially with children, not at all austere, with a lot of charm."

General Panet, who often invited other members to ride with him on his private railroad car, brought his beautiful Irish setter with him and this caused a problem because dogs were not permitted as Mabel Selby Bryson, a member of the dining room staff, remembers: "The great mystery was where General Panet's dog slept. We tried not to know for some of the other members grumbled because pets were not permitted to set a paw in the place." Banty Reid also

General Panet with dog on left; "Povey" Hale on far right (Anne Hale Wonham Collection)

recalls General Panet's beautiful setter: "It was perfectly trained but finally the manager, Leigh Harding, laid down the law – no dogs and no exceptions even for a General, so eventually, I think, Panet dropped out of the Club."

John Fry remembers those pre-war years at the Club which his parents had joined in 1936: "I remember as a child arriving with my family at the train station of Ste-Agathe-des-Monts. In the eerie, sub-Arctic air of nightfall, the steam locomotive hissed and groaned in a manner that I could recall with complete familiarity 30 years later when I first saw the train scenes in *Dr. Zhivago*. Along the station platform horse-drawn sleighs waited to transport arriving passengers to their second homes in the hills or on the shores of a hundred frozen lakes ...

"[The Shawbridge Club] resembled a noisy boarding-house with a learn-to-ski program ... it seemed almost like an extension of the private school, Lower Canada College, which I attended in Montreal, except there were no teachers to cane you if you misbehaved. At the end of a day of skiing and ski-joring, members dined at communal tables.

"In order to learn to ski, of course, we needed a teacher. At the Shawbridge Club, we were led out on the trails by an old Norwegian with piercing eyes and a lean, hard frame angled like a wind-torn bristle-cone pine. Mr. Johannsen was an inspiring mentor ..."

On May 17, 1939, King George VI and his Queen, Elizabeth, sailed into Quebec City to begin their royal tour across Canada, the first British sovereigns to do so. Less than three months later, on September 3, Hitler's panzer divisions rumbled into Poland. "We didn't know it at the time," recalls Bruce Kippen, "but it was the end of an era of skiing in North America with the Shawbridge Club at the very centre."

Royal Tour 1939, Montreal (CPR Collection)

THE GOVERNOR-GENERAL'S VISIT

Soon many of the ski pioneers in the Laurentians showed up in uniform, then embarked for overseas: men like Harry Pangman, the honorary coach of the Red Birds until he left to fight with the Canadian Army in Sicily. Those who enlisted retained their membership in the Shawbridge Club but were exempt from paying dues.

Despite the hostilities, the Club flourished. "People went up there," writes Michael Drummond, "to forget about the war and their losses. I saw one mother sitting quietly in the lounge beside the fireplace; she had just lost a son that week. We lost two cousins about the time of D-day, 1944. Some mothers lost more than one child."

Michael also remembers how much fun it was getting to the Club, even during the war:

"On Friday evening, Mom would drive me to the Park Avenue station. I can still smell the orange peels and the gas lamps on that train and the sharp snap of the cold air when we got to Shawbridge and into Maxwell's sleigh. Then the swish of the sleigh in the snow, the crack of Maxwell's whip and the aroma of the wood smoke curling up from the chimneys of all the houses."

A few months before the outbreak of war, a new development boosted the number of skiers streaming north. Having spent $750,000, Joe Ryan now owned a mountain, a ski tow and an inn, all of which opened for business on February 12, 1939. About a year later, *Time* magazine published a feature article on the Laurentians calling Ryan's Tremblant resort the east coast's answer to Sun Valley. The article brought many skiers from Canada, the United States and further afield, to Tremblant. According to Louise Arbique in *Tremblant,* thousands of guests registered at the resort and it was estimated that the Ryans (Joe had remarried this time to Mary Rutherford, a vivacious Virginian and, like her husband, an excellent skier) were bringing $300,000 in American money alone into the Quebec economy.

Some winter tourists who came to the Laurentians discovered a new fashion sensation. The ski wear of Irving Margolese, the Montreal clothes designer (known simply as "Irving") was all the rage at fashion shows. Louis Cochand (a fashion plate himself) returned from ski races in Poland wearing a dashing pair of ski pants, pleated and easy to move in, the same type he had seen a Polish prince wearing on the slopes. Once he saw them, Irving designed a similar line. All Louis' friends and ski pupils wanted them. Saks Fifth Avenue ordered the pants in quantity. At the Club, ski instructor Mario Gabriel donned a pair. No doubt, the ski pants helped make Irving an international celebrity associated with Daryl Zanuck, Howard Hughes, and the fashion editors of *Vogue* and *Harper's* magazines.

After the war, celebrities from all over the world – Crown Prince Bernhard of the Netherlands, Jacqueline Bouvier Kennedy, Henry Ford – came to Joe Ryan's mountain. Robert and Ethel Kennedy met each other on the slopes which Herman Johannsen had helped Joe set out. Sometimes skiers from the Shawbridge Club rented a bus and skied on Tremblant. Occasionally they would see Joe, in the words of Louise Arbique, "a handsome, merry, and elegant man, outside the lodge, wearing a cashmere coat with a velvet collar and a Kavanaugh, the hat of the rich and the powerful."

But there was a dark and disquieting side to the beetle-browed "golden skier". Joe Ryan drank too much, had a volcanic temper that often erupted even out on the hills, and he spent money that he didn't have to expand his mountain empire.

Some of his associates and friends became increasingly concerned about Ryan's volatile personality, wondering where it would all end. Early in the fall of 1950, Jim Ware (later a member of the Shawbridge Club with his wife, Garnice), travelled to Mont-Tremblant to discuss insurance matters with Joe. Ryan refused to see him, a snub conveyed by his secretary.

But while he waited, Jim Ware could hear Ryan through a partition shouting and cursing at members of the resort staff. A short time later Ryan travelled to New York and checked into a hotel. On the afternoon of September 12, 1950 his broken body was found on the sidewalk beneath his hotel window. Joe Ryan had fallen to his death. There was shock and sadness

Mario Gabriel at the front door of the Club wearing Irving's famous Polish pants (Frances Williams Collection)

Paulette Goddard; Burgess Meredith, her husband and Irving of Montreal at the 1948 St. Moritz Olympics. Daryl Zanuck flew Irving over to provide sportswear for some of his film stars. The Canadian Olympic skiers wore Irving designs

(Canadian Ski Museum Collection)

at the Shawbridge Club at the tragic loss of a man who had done so much for the Laurentians and with whom some of the members had skied on his beloved mountain.

Windsor Station in wartime (CPR Collection)

Even those members who stayed at the Club during the war years kept an eye and an ear on the conflict, especially those who had loved ones overseas. They were shocked at the attack by the Japanese on Pearl Harbor on December 7, 1941, an attack that brought the United States into the war. They were buoyed three weeks later as they gathered around the Club's radio to listen to Winston Churchill's electrifying speech to a joint session of the Canadian Parliament. Shortly before his address, Vichy France's political leaders, having thrown in the towel themselves, predicted that Britain would have its neck wrung like a chicken. Churchill looked at the Canadian parliamentarians and growled, "Some chicken, some neck!"

Like all other Canadians, Club members prayed and held their breath as 175,000 soldiers – a significant number of them Canadians – splashed ashore on the Normandy beaches on June 6, 1944. Almost a year later, on May 8, 1945 – VE day – they, with other Canadians, celebrated Hitler's defeat with bells, bonfires, impromptu parades, tumultuous parties and religious services.

For members who had fought overseas, the Club was an invigorating haven after the war. Andrea Rutherford Burgess fondly recalls her father's experience. Andy Rutherford, who had played football for McGill, served as a Lieutenant-Colonel with the Royal Canadian Engineers. "When he returned in 1945," his daughter writes, "the Club was his saving grace. After seeing so much destruction, just to be able to go up north and ski and relax with friends at the Club as his two older brothers did after the First World War – well, I think it was the reason Dad survived that post-war period so well."

Colonel Rutherford also participated in a highlight of the post-war period at the Club, the first visit by a Governor-General. Earl Alexander of Tunis, one of Canada's most popular Governors-General, was a genuine military hero who had led the Allied forces in the Mediterranean theatre. His Excellency was on a short visit to Montreal in March, 1947, when one of his honorary Montreal A.D.Cs, Air Vice-Marshal Frank S. McGill, a Club member, suggested to Alexander – a good skier himself – that he might enjoy driving up to the Shawbridge Club for a visit and a turn on the slopes.

Air Vice-Marshall Frank McGill founded and led the only Canadian Squadron to fly in the Battle of Britain – Westmount's 401.

(Mrs. Frank McGill Collection)

When the Governor-General's party arrived, they changed into ski togs and Mario Gabriel, the instructor with the sun glasses and the dark tan, took them to a nearby hill for some skiing. Colonel Rutherford, also a capable skier, was part of the group that returned to the Club for a quiet drink in the lounge.

Just before going into the dining room for Sunday luncheon, Isabel McGill (Cameron) was summoned by her father:

"Dad took the Governor-General up to Shawbridge to the Club to ski. At lunch time, he said to me, 'You will have to curtsy for him.' 'But Dad,' I said, 'I have my ski boots on and I can't take them off.' (In those days, we didn't take our ski boots off as they were heavy leather with straps; we ate lunch in them.) 'Never mind, Isabel, you must make a curtsy with your boots on.' So, I made my little bob and the G.G. didn't seem to notice! But I have never forgotten it!"

The Governor-General, who visited the Club on March 23, 1947, just missed that winter's most ferocious snowstorm, a blizzard that saw more than 2,000 skiers stranded for the night at Ste-Rose and that made the cover of *Life* magazine. Michael Drummond remembers taking shelter under the pool table in the hotel in Ste-Rose. One of the few members who managed to catch the only train that got through to Montreal was Andrea Rutherford Burgess – a lucky thing, because she was due for an appendix operation. Next day, the Club struck an emergency committee to make coffee and sandwiches for those who failed to find shelter.

Earl Alexander of Tunis (Canadian Ski Museum Collection)

During these early post-war years, the Club was usually filled to overflowing. One of the reasons was easier transportation, particularly the growing use of automobiles to travel to the Laurentians even in winter. Shortly after the outbreak of the war, route 11, now the Rue Principale in Shawbridge, was opened for winter traffic. Then Curé Labelle Highway, route 117, was also opened for use in winter.

CNR Schedule 1934-35. Mrs. Marshall's and the Laurentian Lodge are listed under Shawbridge

(Brodie Shearer Collection)

This was a great improvement on the time three gas-driven contraptions had scared the farmers and their cows on the St-Hippolyte road in 1914. An improvement, too, over one of the first times Banty Reid struggled to reach Shawbridge by car:

"In the spring of 1932 I drove up to Shawbridge with a girl friend to go skiing. All of a sudden the road ended at St-Jérôme. There seemed to be some kind of track ahead, not much more than a cowpath. I thought this girl knew her way so I took her advice and ploughed ahead in the snowy track.

"Half-way to Shawbridge I looked up and saw three cars bearing down on us. 'Oh hell!' I thought. I quickly drove into a farmer's yard which had been ploughed out. Then I looked back and there were three more cars coming from St-Jérôme. 'This will be interesting,' I thought. Before you knew it six guys from the six cars charged out, lifted up three cars like three boxes of chocolates, and set them on the side of the road. We all continued serenely on our way in both directions and my lady friend and I made it safely to Shawbridge."

It was not just the parlous state of the roads that discouraged the war-time use of cars but also gas-rationing. Although there were exceptions, as Anne Henry Murdoch notes:

"During the war when gasoline was strictly rationed, we only rarely drove to Shawbridge. I do, however, remember a few occasions when we splurged and went up by car. Beyond St-Jérôme there was no winter maintenance of the highway, so some enterprising farmers ploughed a road through their fields and collected tolls." Others made it to the Club by car in war-time.

Herbie Lewis recalls on one occasion "we were so eager to get to the Club for the weekend that my date, Cynthia Hands (later to become my wife) and I went to a deb dance with our long underwear under our evening clothes so that we could make a fast get-away after the party to drive up to the Club."

D-10 number 1088 rumbles through heavy winter storm near Piedmont (CPR Collection)

Anne Murdoch found that nothing much had changed in the Club's war-time routine:

"When the trains came in to the CPR station, they were met by a big sleigh drawn by Percherons. It was wonderful to load our skis and knapsacks onto the sleigh and jump in to snuggle under huge buffalo rugs, listening to the bells on the horses' collars as we were driven up the front drive lined with trees (and lights at Christmas time) to the front door. There were ski racks all along the walls of the big verandah where we would leave our skis.

"After the day's skiing there was the smell of the wet woollen clothing hanging out to dry on the hooks along the walls of the main hall. After the skiers were home, either from the Big Hill or some other trail like 'the Fallen Women', we would order a tea tray to be brought to us in the lovely lounge with its blazing fire. There we would relax, fill ourselves with hot buttered toast and strawberry jam and talk about our day's adventures."

The "Chief" and Alice were also nearby during the war years (Herman had tried to volunteer but, ironically, failed to pass the medical.) "The Johannsens", writes Anne Murdoch, "lived in a house reached by a path across the fields behind the Club. Much traffic travelled back and forth on that path. Mr. and Mrs. Johannsen were the sort of people who attracted the young and they were always welcoming when we knocked on their door. I often wonder how Mrs. Johannsen coped with us, so often turning up for tea after a day of skiing, or just dropping in to check with them on our way home."

These were the years, the Thirties and the Forties, when the Shawbridge Club hit its stride. It was open for business seven days a week; in 1947 there were 150 members and another twenty-five day members. The staff of twelve under the well-liked and capable Leigh Harding numbered a chef, Harry Lawton, a pastry chef, a bartender and several waiters and nearly always

(CPR Collection)

included one or more members of the Selby family from Shawbridge. There was a friendly relationship between the village and the Club, marked by ski meets and festivities.

Special ski weeks were laid on in February and March. Mr. Harding would send the overflow to the Maple Leaf Inn or to Mrs. Marshall's boarding-house.

"My parents," writes Natalie Harding, "saw a lot of Mrs. Marshall. They were good friends. She would come over to the Club when Mother invited the Ladies' Aid at the church to High Tea. My parents would go over to her boarding-house. I remember it had a large verandah. Mrs. Marshall was warm and welcoming, not too large with darkish hair. We'd see her regularly at the church suppers, one of which was held at the Club."

Most weekends there was no extra room at the Club even though the young people had their own quarters – the young men at the Boys' Club, a house at the foot of the Big Hill, where they cooked their own breakfast and lunch and quaffed a few beers and the girls at their own house just down the road. Once when one of the male members tried to crash the Girls' Club, the ever-vigilant matron promptly gave him the boot.

Nineteen forty-eight was the year that Barbara Ann Scott won Canada's first Olympic gold medal for figure skating and Louis St-Laurent succeeded Mackenzie King as prime minister.

There had been some changes at the golf club over the years. Having leased club premises from the Ski Club in 1924, the directors of the golf club refused to accept a higher rental, so they bought a farm behind the fourth green and the farmhouse became their new

Les Perry, artist, architect and gentleman at spring sugaring off
(Nemec family Collection)

clubhouse. This arrangement collapsed with the onset of the Depression and the golfers returned to using the facilities of the Ski Club. Their main source of revenue during the war years were the green fees paid by members of the Ski Club and by guests at the Maple Leaf Inn.

There were also some changes and renovations at the Shawbridge Club, often involving the suggestions of Les Perry, an architect and one of the Club's most popular and thoughtful members. Les could be seen every morning carrying up a breakfast tray to his wife, Edith. He was also often seen beside a stand of pine or on a snowy knoll overlooking a little white church, seated on a canvas chair, his palette in front of him, painting the Laurentian landscape. Les Perry, whom I came to regard with much affection, always got a kick out of recounting how in 1848 his great-grandfather, Alfred Perry, had helped sack and burn Montreal's Parliament Buildings on Youville Square to protest giving compensation to those who had rebelled against the Crown in 1837. Les relished the irony that his great-grandfather was a fireman.

The Thirties and Forties, highlighted by the visit of the Governor-General, Earl Alexander of Tunis, were halcyon days at the Club and there were more to come.

"THE GENTLE GIANT"

There was no lovelier season at the Shawbridge Club than Christmas and New Year's – a time for holiday skiing, games, songs and family fun. Virginia Birks Alexandor looks back:

"New Year's Eve parties – with a sleigh ride, music, games and paper hats; so many old friends – the Currie, Penfield, Lindsay and Henry families, Bill Notman, Michael Drummond – to name only a very few. Jolly Mr. Harding at the reception desk; spying on bath tub occupants through the little broken piece in the wall; ping-pong tournaments – all so long ago! There was a friendly, easy ambience and camaraderie about the Shawbridge Club which is a precious memory today."

Doctor Wilder Penfield (Kate Williams Collection)

Allan Turner Bone describes "Murray Badgely's power with the pipes on so many New Year's Eve parties, when the crowd would march up one stairs and down the other, while the piper called the tune, and Jerry Johnston provided drinks as they passed him on the stairs." Poppy Welsford McClure recalls, "winding through the house, hands on each others' shoulders in a snake line." Anne Murdoch writes of the special guests during the Christmas holiday period like Jean Vanier, founder of the L' Arche homes for the mentally challenged, and his brother, likely the guests of General Panet and his wife who were renting a house across the road from the Club. "Jean Vanier would have been in his teens and a university student at the time."

There were also high jinks on New Year's Eve. During the war Bruce Kippen, on leave from the RCAF base at Trenton, stopped at the famous St-Sauveur Pub where he had started drinking at the ripe old age of thirteen: "Wing Commander 'Chink' Walker was leading the lusty singing of 'Scarlet O'Hara, the Pride of the South' and 'Nine Old Ladies Locked in the Lavatory', a traditional ski-train ballad."

George Currie also remembers being allowed to go to the St-Sauveur Pub for the first time on New Year's Eve when he was just sixteen: "Some chap drank a whole bedpan of beer in one long quaff; we returned on skis to the Club after midnight in the moonlight – a foolhardy adventure!"

When Kirk McLeod was president of the Club on New Year's Eve, 1935, several of his friends came to the party in a horse and cutter. They tied the horse outside to a post on the verandah and went in to enjoy the festivities. As the party inside reached a crescendo, some charitable member thought the horse might like a drink. However, President McLeod and Eddie Renouf, chairman of the house committee, concluded the real problem was that the horse wanted to join the party inside. So to manager Leigh Harding's horror, the president, Eddie and others, with much huffing and puffing, tried to push and pull horse and sleigh through the front door. To many cheers, they shoved the horse through but the sleigh was too wide and when the wide-eyed horse lunged round and bit President Kirk in the buttocks, they thought better of it and went inside for another drink themselves.

Swing and sway with Rodolphe and Jean Carignan and Bob Hill, 1954
(Bob Hill Collection)

There was music and dancing, much of it square dancing. "There was always a mob at New Year's," recalls John Trim, "Don Baillie would play the violin and Fred Gross used to play the piano with a towel over it." But the music at the Club was about to change. At the end of the Forties, two classmates at Westhill High School teamed up to play for square dances which suddenly became more popular in 1949 when the Governor-General, still Earl Alexander of Tunis, hosted a square dance at Rideau Hall for Princess Elizabeth on a visit to Ottawa.

Bob Hill played the guitar and Donald MacSween did the calling. In 1950, Boyd Millen invited them to do the New Year's party

New Year's Eve at the Club with Bob Hill and dancers, Ann and Albert Nixon
(L.L.C. Collection)

at the Club. Leigh Harding paid them fifteen dollars each – their first hard cash. As a magical bonus, Bob Hill also brought a quiet man, Jean Carignan, who would become Quebec's most famous fiddler, to the Club for several New Year's parties. "He came to the Club with me and was an instant hit with the members."

Obviously, Bob Hill could have earned far more money on New Year's Eve playing larger and fancier halls. There was only room on the floor in the Club lounge for four sets at one time: "But I had earned my first money at the Club. When they asked me back, I was more than glad to go. It was much nicer than run-of-the-mill parties. The Club was one of the rare places where parents and teenagers could have a good time together at the same party. And it folded up at a decent hour because everyone was keen to get out skiing the next day." Bob Hill continued to play at the Club on New Year's Eve for thirty years and hosted his own square dance program on CJAD; and Donald MacSween gained fame with McGill's sensational revue, "My Fur Lady"; and Jean Carignan travelled around the world with Pete Seeger, played before the Queen, and became a fixture at major Quebec events.

Besides the music and dancing, there were other New Year's traditions at the Club. Karin Austin O'Gorman ("Jackrabbit's" granddaughter) remembers the oldest member bringing the youngest member to the party:

"My mother tells the story of Hugh Harrigan bringing me to the Club as the New Year's baby when I was eighteen months. For years after that, Hugh, a bachelor, would send us children incredible gifts at Christmas, like some magical Santa Claus, or if he ran out of ideas, he would send a cheque that would allow me to buy something I would never have been able to afford. This continued until Hugh died when I was about sixteen."

When midnight approached on New Year's Eve, Mme. Panet had her own ritual as Anne Murdoch remembers: "She used to take a broom and sweep the whole of the main hallway, arriving at the front door just at midnight. Then she would open the door, sweep out the dust of the old year and open the door wide to welcome the New Year in." Then the custom was to join hands in front of the fireplace, count down to midnight, 'Auld Lang Syne', cheers and

Jim Hugessen as the reporter in My Fur Lady

(Photo June Sauer; McCord Museum of Canadian History, Montreal)

hugs all round, champagne followed by more dancing, this time to the velvety radio music of Guy Lombardo and his Royal Canadians.

Doctors Peter Lehman, Wilder Penfield and Frans McNaughton c. 1944

(Penfield Archives, Osler Library, McGill University)

One of the more memorable New Year's Eve celebrations at the Shawbridge Club occurred on December 31, 1952 when the members, clustered around the radio, heard that Queen Elizabeth had awarded the Order of Merit to Dr. Wilder Penfield. Bill Feindel, a close associate of Wilder Penfield, and a member of the Shawbridge Club along with Faith, his wife, sums up his colleague: "Penfield was a pioneer in working on human brain function and on brain mapping at the Montreal Neurological Institute, which he founded. He explored and was the first to identify the areas of the brain that controlled speech and memory, areas which had not previously been known."

Wilder Penfield, born in Spokane, Washington, in 1891, came to Montreal from New York in 1928 and shortly afterwards, as he writes in his moving autobiography, *No Man Alone,* he and his family were introduced to skiing: "My wife and I were initiated into the sport of skiing and soon we organized a skiing weekend for my Princeton classmates ... at the Chalet Cochand in Sainte-Marguerite, Quebec."

In 1929, the Penfields bought two deserted farms on Lake Memphremagog – not far from the Hermitage Club where they sometimes stayed – which would become their summer home. In the winter of 1930, Penfield describes skiing on the lake behind a light sleigh driven by Erick Jackson who would manage the farm property:

"When [Jackson] started home, we put on our skis and ski-jored behind him far out on that magnificent lake, which extends thirty-two miles from Magog in Quebec southward to Newport in Vermont. These are the lovely highlands of what is called the Eastern Townships of Quebec, les Cantons de l'Est.

"The sun was setting as we dropped the ski-jor ropes and waved goodbye to Jackson. Warm colour had come to the snowy plain. Our skis carried us smoothly back toward the Hermitage, shish, shish, shish, while a sense of peace and strength came to us ..."

That same winter, 1930, Wilder Penfield and his family joined the Shawbridge Club, introduced by Cleveland Dodge, who had been their neighbour in Riverdale-on-Hudson, in Westchester county, New York. Dr. Penfield was one of the first at breakfast to answer the "Chief's" piercing call, "Who's for skiing this morning? All out!" And Dr. Penfield adds, "How disappointed we who brought our children and ourselves to this homely ski club would have been had he not come each morning."

Dr. Penfield's children (he had four) had their own warm relationship with "Jackrabbit". Jeff Penfield recalls him leading "an enthusiastic group of boys" on an overnight jaunt to

Dr. Penfield with three of his children, Ruthmary, Jeff and Wilder Jr. (Kate Williams Collection)

Tremblant. At the end of the Thirties, Priscilla Penfield was bed-ridden for more than a year with a pre-tubercular condition. When she recovered and returned to the Club, she was concerned that the skiing skills of her peers had improved so much beyond hers:

"My father knew I dreaded even to join them in ski class on the Big Hill so Daddy cooked up a plan with Mr. Johannsen for the three of us to meet early before breakfast one morning and to slip out alone on skis to the Practice Hill. It was barely light, but he coached me on the way to recover the easy slide-slide and when I gasped Oh dear! at the top of the hill, he said, 'Don't worry, traverse is easy, weight on the downhill ski, uphill ski ahead. Simple!' And it was. Finally, back at the top, he urged me, 'straight down now, you'll love it.' And I did. One little session from those wonderful role models and I was ready to join my friends. I went back to breakfast elated and Daddy and Mr. Johannsen they kept my secret."

The war years were difficult for the Penfields as they were for most Canadian families. In December, 1942, Penfield writes that the family had gone up to the Laurentians for some "skiing in the sun, then tea at the Club in the glow from the cold and climbing, and home in the car singing all the way." That year the Christmas holiday was especially poignant because on December 27, Dr. Penfield was standing on the platform at Windsor Station watching his eldest son, Wilder Jr., leave for active service: "Towering above the crowd, with his beret at a rakish angle, knapsack over one shoulder and swagger stick under his arm, he looked altogether splendid ..."

What many remember about the Penfield family at the Club was their joie-de-vivre and musical ability. "Dr. Penfield was an unassuming quiet man," writes Anne Murdoch. "I knew Jeff and Priscilla. Jeff joined the choir at Princeton and he would lead barbershop, we would all sing around the piano." Her brother, John Henry, also recalls the singing: "One happy New Year's Eve, a quartet made up of Jeff Penfield, Wilder Penfield Sr. and me and one other, probably Hugh Wallis, rehearsed and sang 'Cool, Clear Water' in glorious harmony to entertain the gathered throng." Bob Hill, from his orchestra vantage point, spotted Dr. Penfield: "There was one guy who was always the first one up on the dance floor with his wife. After a couple of years it dawned on me this was Wilder Penfield whom I knew by reputation. He was an avid square dancer."

At the beginning of the Fifties, Wilder Penfield, tall and trim, sometimes called "the gentle giant", was at the height of his powers, a Montreal neurosurgeon held in great regard in medical circles around the world. In January 1951, surrounded by friends and colleagues from the Neurological Institute, he celebrated his sixtieth birthday, described by his biographer as "a gala event" at the Shawbridge Club. And the following year, December 31, 1952 he was again at the Club when it was announced on the radio that the Queen had awarded him the Order of Merit, the only civilian honour that Winston Churchill would accept at the end of the war.

So it was that in June, 1953, Dr. Penfield and his wife, Helen (to whom he always carried a breakfast tray to her room at the Club), sailed for England, attended the Coronation in Westminister Abbey, accepted honorary degrees from Oxford and Cardiff Universities and at a Ceremony at Buckingham Palace on the morning of July 7, presided over by the new Queen, was awarded his decoration, a red cross with golden letters which read, 'For Merit'. It was a milestone in the distinguished career of "the gentle giant".

Douglas McCurdy at controls of the Silver Dart (Alexander Graham Bell Museum, Baddeck, N.S.)

CELEBRITIES

Wilder Penfield was not the only member of the Shawbridge Club whose name and reputation were widely known. Bruce Kippen recalls J.A.D (Douglas) McCurdy who was the first man in Canada to fly an aeroplane:

"About 1936, 1 remember being kept awake hearing the old bucks, my father and Douglas McCurdy (then aged fifty) of flying fame, singing World War One songs like 'It's a long way to Tipperary' and 'Has Anyone Here Seen Kelly?' Douglas McCurdy had a big deep voice that shook the rafters. He was an energetic masculine guy, the first man in the British Empire to fly a plane, the Silver Dart, on February 23, 1909, with Alexander Graham Bell looking on. That was six years after the Wright brothers. By the time he joined the Shawbridge Club, he had founded his own aircraft company, and later, in 1947, he was appointed Lieutenant-Governor of Nova Scotia."

Indeed so close was Douglas McCurdy to Alexander Graham Bell and his wife that after his own mother died when he was a teenager, the Bells considered adopting him. In 1907 Bell engaged four young engineers, one being Douglas, to help build a successful flying machine at Baddeck, Nova Scotia, where Douglas grew up.

And it was Douglas that Bell chose to attempt the first airplane flight in Canada. On a cold winter day, February 23, 1909, a horse-drawn sleigh drew the plane, named the *Silver Dart,* across a frozen lake with Douglas at the controls. Hordes of children (school had been let out for the day) skated behind this curious machine. Men helped point the *Silver Dart* into the wind and cranked the propeller. Douglas revved the engine and when it sounded all right, he tore down the icy surface and the machine lifted into the air. The school children chased him on their skates, and the townspeople stared in disbelief as the *Silver Dart* reached the unbelievable height of thirty feet and flew nearly a mile at forty miles an hour.

Years later when Douglas joined the Shawbridge Club, did he find in skiing something of the same soaring freedom he had discovered in flying? Others, like Saint-Exupéry in *Terre des Hommes,* have written of being borne on wings towards the limitless horizon. Perhaps flying through the mountains on skis, the wind in his face, the sun dancing on the powdered snow, the graceful glides through nature's wonderland, gave Douglas something of what he felt the first time he sailed above that frozen lake in the *Silver Dart.*

(Cartoon by Betty Maxwell, courtesy Penguin Ski Club)

Another distinguished flyer, Air Vice-Marshal Frank McGill, was also a long-time member of the Club. He founded and led the only Canadian squadron to fight in the Battle of Britain – Westmount's 401 squadron – and he arranged for the Governor-General, Earl Alexander of Tunis, to ski at the Club after the war. His obituary, in 1980, concluded that no one had "more faithfully and more stalwartly stood on guard for Canada."

Another prominent Montrealer, Charlie Peters, who would become editor of *The Gazette,* was a popular member of the Club in the Fifties. While at McGill he was nearly expelled for kidnapping a student who had refused to stand during the playing of God Save The King. In 1940, Charlie Peters was among those who connived to have Mayor Camillien Houde arrested for opposing the war effort. (When Houde was released and easily re-elected mayor of Montreal, he and Peters became friends.)

Charlie Peters, a more graceful writer than a skier, was given to expressing himself in verse which he did in 1953 when he joined a bus trip from the Club to ski on Tremblant. It was a long poem entitled "A Sissy on the Schuss", of which a few stanzas will suffice for our purposes:

"As a somewhat timid skier
I'd been suffering great abuse.
So I thought I'd show my courage
On the lightning Sissy Schuss.

So I leaped upon the chair-tow
Hanging on with all my might
Hoping no one would remark that
I was petrified with fright.

At the top the veteran Andy
Gaily said: 'Just follow me.
There is really nothing to it
Almost anyone can ski.'

So I started bravely downward
Crash – I came down heavily
All piled up in great confusion
Skis and poles and tuque and me.

Allan Turner Bone came by me
Skiing like a bird in flight
'No one here should ski like you, son
Somebody will think you're tight'...

So I pulled myself together
Though my knees were out of line
Banty laughed as he sailed downward
'Come along, the skiing's fine.'

Then I saw a boulder looming
Just as large as old Mount Royal
And I wrapped myself around it
Like an ancient battery coil...

Here's the moral of this story
Of these brilliant skiers beware
No more Sissy Schuss for me, friends,
From now on I'm skiing with Clare."

The Valley of the Fallen Women, 1928.
"Hugie" Knatchbull-Hugessen (second from right) with Eileen Russel, Andy Rutherford, Lyle Williams, Peggy Hugessen and Norah Hodgson, (standing Lindsay Hall)

(Frances Williams Collection)

The Shawbridge Club also had its share of politicians, elected and unelected. Senator Adrian Knatchbull-Hugessen, born in Kent, England, went to McGill, served with the Canadian Expeditionary Force in World War One and practised law in Montreal as did his son, Jim, who later became a Justice on the Federal Court in Ottawa. Both were long-time members of the Club. The Senator's middle name, Knatchbull, twigged the interest of the children who had fun (and difficulty) trying to pronounce it. Brooke Claxton was a minister in two Liberal governments, those of Mackenzie King and Louis St-Laurent. A keen skier, he later became the first chairman of the Canada Council. Senator Landon Mackenzie Pearson writes of the influence of the Club:

"One thing I do know is that I owe my profound attachment to the Province of Quebec in part to my happy excursions into the Laurentians and my days in the agreeable atmosphere of the Club. That physical attachment was later enhanced after I learned French and acquired a number of intimate Quebec friends ... I have come to appreciate how much Quebec, in all its aspects, is part of who I am as a Canadian. Never underestimate the power of place!"

Over the years, too, no fewer than four mayors of Westmount joined the Club which has a code of unwritten rules, one of which – no discussing politics or religion – was seldom breached.

"Jackrabbit" and friends (Peggy Johannsen Austin Collection)

Naturally, the Club had many outstanding skiers, Percy Douglas, "Jackrabbit" himself and Harry Pangman to name three. One of the peaks at Tremblant was named for Johannsen, another for Pangman. The Club had strong women skiers, some of them also members of the Penguins. There was Barbara Kemp, a tall sturdy woman, whose first love was horses and riding, followed closely by skiing.

Barbara (whom my wife Catharine and I got to know when we joined the Club in 1974 and who was still skiing in the year 2000) remembers riding with her sister, Betty, across Mount Royal on an icy cold day in November, 1933, when they noticed far below them "the glint of sun on a steel-blue carriage, and we heard the boom boom of big guns. It was the funeral procession of Sir Arthur Currie, the much loved principal of McGill, who had led Canadian forces in the war, a turning point in Canada's history. The horses had a terrible time dragging that heavy gun carriage up the mountain from University Avenue to the Protestant Cemetery."

Barbara Kemp laid out the equestrian course at Bromont in Quebec's Eastern Townships for the 1976 Olympic games: "I lived in Bromont for months. First, I skied the whole terrain. Some people thought I was out of my depth but the local men building the obstacles were on my side and so was Prince Philip whose daughter, Princess Anne, would be jumping them: 'We know you think it's rideable,' teased the Prince one morning, 'because you've skied it.'"

Once in the Thirties, Barbara Kemp and Barbara MacTaggart decided to spend the night on the top of Mont-Tremblant, in the Wheeler's old place, the White Peak Cabin. They climbed up, then skied over to the cabin only to find "it was already occupied by twenty boisterous boys on a stag party knocking back Kandahar cocktails, a mixture of straight alcool, pine needles and snow." So the young ladies prudently decided to sleep outside but close to the cabin. Barbara

Kemp tells what happened then: "I woke with a start at two in the morning and found myself staring into two pairs of gleaming eyes. A pair of wolves were between us and the cabin. We held our breath until two boys came out of the cabin for a smoke and the wolves vanished into the night."

Ken Farmer, another long-time member and still active, had early on made his name as one of the best hockey players ever to skate for McGill. Years later, when I skied with him and his wife, Lorrayne (a very graceful skier), I noticed that Ken's favourite way of stopping on a helter-skelter hill was to head straight for the nearest tree. After the inevitable collision, Ken would struggle out of the deep snow, straighten his skis and carry on.

Of course, 'Jackrabbit' himself was still going strong in the Forties and Fifties, still showing up at many a morning breakfast to get a good start on the day. Anne Murdoch describes the scene:

"Don't we remember awaiting his arrival while we ate our breakfast, waiting eagerly for his suggestion about which trail to take? He'd tell us how far we would be skiing (the Johannsen miles were very long) and we'd need to order a lunch or at least the makings for something to cook over a fire. The Chief's husky, Nicki, would be harnessed to a sled and would pull much of the load for the rest of us. Jackrabbit would spring ahead, way ahead of us, and would find us a suitable place to stop to make our lunch and might even have had a fire started in the snow before we could catch up with him."

Faith and Bill Feindel (a close associate of Dr. Penfield and later Director of the Neurological Institute) also remember:

Dinner at the Club's sixtieth anniversary, April 9, 1983
(l. to r.) Frank Nemec; Ken Farmer; Herb and Lois McLean; Ian and Marg. Mair (standing); Marjorie Reid (partially hidden); Banty Reid; Tubby Rollit; "Van" Wagner; Ann and Albert Nixon (president); "Jackrabbit"; Norma Rollit; Charles Peters ("A Sissy on the Schuss") and Elaine Peters. (L.L.C. Collection)

"One sunny spring morning when the snow was still deep on the fields and in the nearby woods, 'Jackrabbit' came along with me and my two small sons and patiently showed them how to cross small streams and get over barbed wire without removing their skis. One would never guess from the time and care he spent on that little trip that he was the great developer of skiing in the Laurentians."

During the Forties and Fifties, the Club also kept up its indoor activities. Banty Reid says Lois McLean organized games, painting and handicrafts: "Her most memorable project was an annual costume ball on Friday of ski week and it was always a big success." Sometimes the children overdid things and Mr. Harding would lay down the law especially if there were complaints from the "old fuds" as Bruce Kippen called them: "Once, because my billiard cue had cut the green felt on the pool table and then, at supper, when all hell broke loose at the children's table after Elizabeth Henry tossed a bun at me causing Mr. Harding to take drastic action and we were bodily removed from the dining room." Herbie Lewis remembers with relief graduating from the children's table "when we were old enough to have legal cocktails in the lounge before dinner with the wonderful fireplace roaring, and stories of the day's skiing."

Dinner at the Shawbridge Club combined a blend of formality (everyone dressed including the children) and fun (volunteers for after-dinner jokes became a tradition with Allan Turner Bone famous for his frequent stories on "Bossy", the cow). Hugh Seybold summarizes the evening drill: "We would stop skiing about 4:30 in the afternoon, have a shower or a bath followed by a nap, drink from 6 to 7 in the lounge, then go into dinner where someone at your table would buy a bottle of wine (from the bar) and the party continued from there."

Occasionally the party could become high-spirited. Nancy Birks Hale remembers one New Year's "Douglas McCurdy of *Silver Dart* fame crashing down the hallway in noisy high spirits – my first experience, through thin walls, of inebriation!" And there were other indiscretions. "Once," Banty Reid recall, "Mrs. Wilder Penfield arrived downstairs in the middle of the night and sternly informed a frightened young couple, 'There is no necking in the dining room.'"

Some, like Hugh Wallis, were of a more cerebral bent: "Many a Saturday evening after dinner we would have great philosophical chats with Leigh Harding in his wicket beside the bar. The conversations were helped by the greatest whisky sours in the world ably prepared by Ray, the bartender."

Invariably, the weekend came to a close and it was time to head home. John Trim has "a vague memory of adults drinking hot rum toddies waiting for the train back to Montreal. Then on the train, strangers standing on the wicker seats , trying to blow out the gas lanterns. You would give a good blow, and then everyone would settle down. It was just part of the fun of going home after a great weekend at the Club."

CHANGES

Flying Skis, Taylor Kennedy, 1932. (Kennedy Family Collection)

Right from its beginnings, the Shawbridge Club attracted Americans. The name of Samuel Alexander Stephens, the manufacturer from Lynn, Massachusetts (from whose family the Club was purchased) was on the document attesting to the Club's incorporation in 1924. Another early member, also from Massachusetts, was George Cabot, forever linked to that other aristocratic Boston family, the Lowells, who spoke only to the Cabots who spoke only to God. Cleveland Dodge, a businessman associated with the Phelps-Dodge copper company, was a member as were his children and eventually his grandchildren. It was "Clee" Dodge who introduced Wilder Penfield to the Club, another American who held dual citizenship. Members of the Chrysler family came from New York. And a frequent guest about 1929 was Dr. Irving Langmuir from Schenectady, New York, the winner of the Nobel Prize for Chemistry in 1932. In 1945, after "Jackrabbit's" son, Bob, escaped from Nazi-occupied Norway where he had been studying, Dr. Langmuir gave him a position at the General Electric plant in Schenectady. Bruce Kippen and others remember the Nobel Prize-winner teaching them to ski on the Big Hill.

Space was at a premium during the Fifties and often Leigh Harding would direct the overflow to places just down the road like the Maple Leaf Inn which during this period burnt to the ground one night in a spectacular blaze still vivid for Andrea Rutherford Burgess: "I remember sitting at the window watching the glow, people coming and going with blankets and food, marvelling that the Hays' house next door did not go up as well. It was an image that remained with me long after so I'd have to summon up the picture of a picnic, a nice image to replace it."

The Boys' and Girls' Clubs were also crowded. Anne Murdoch remembers that "the girls were housed in a rather primitive house just along the road from the main Club while the Boys' Club was in a rented house near the base of the Big Hill." Geoffrey Lehman describes something of the goings on there:

The Boys' Club, New Year's 1948. (l. to r.) George Currie, Gordon Fisher, John Fisher, (not identified), Ian Hyde, John Boa, Ken Hague. (Ken Hague Collection)

"We lived in the shack at the bottom of the Big Hill. We cooked our own breakfast and the place was a kind of a mess. In the afternoon as it got dark, we would ski across the river over to the Club. We went down to the basement locker room where we took showers and changed for dinner in the Club. After dinner, we would play ping-pong for a while, then a bunch of us, boys and girls, would go out somewhere, usually to a place in Shawbridge called 'The Snake Pit', whatever its real name was. There we would have a few drinks, dance to the jukebox and just enjoy the evening. Then we'd head back to the Club with a tingling sense of good feeling, change back into our ski clothes in the downstairs locker and ski back to the shack across the river, probably around midnight. It was pitch dark but the cold air on a clear night was exhilarating, the stars wonderfully bright because artificial light was minimal in those days. There was no autoroute, no houses on the Big Hill, only the small lights from the sparse cottages and farmhouses."

Bart Reilly recalls a publishing venture out of the Boys' Shack: "Bob Zeller came up with the idea of *The Shawbridgian*, when we were both at the Boys' Shack. It was a quarterly magazine with blue covers, eight by eleven pages. Several of us went out and got the stories, then put the blasted thing together in someone's basement. We had stories of all the events the Juniors organized: spring races, fun days on the old course, cross-country, funny ski races for the kids.

"We wrote up the torchlight parade when twenty-five of us would go to the top of the mountain, then ski down carrying toilet paper dipped in kerosene attached to poles that wouldn't burn. It took us about a minute and a half to come down, quite a spectacular sight.

"When we Juniors were at the party age, we were allowed to have our own room in the basement under the dining room. I brought my stereo, and we hung out and danced to rock and roll. This was in the late Fifties. Our gang used to get into a lot of trouble. We ran up a horrendously big bar bill, whiskey sours, and so on. We never went in to the first sitting at dinner; and thought nothing of driving with a few drinks, and heading out to the Inn at St-Sauveur that later burned down. Some of us were members of the Island City Singers. We later sang at Expo and came close to going professional.

"I walked into the Club last summer (1999) and it was as though time had not moved, as though I had walked into an old black and white movie: the same old creaky stairs, the bar lined with bottles, the fireplace dominating the same lounge, as comfortable as an old shoe. My wife said, 'Are you all right?' I couldn't answer. Even the old posts for our block heater were still there. I've been out of the Club since 1965. Lots of us grew up there. We had one heck of a good time."

Boyd Whittall recalls when he was still a denizen of the Boys' Club, "My Karen Bulow knitted Sedbergh school tie (with a small identifying mark) went missing." Some years later when Boyd was on the board of the Shawbridge Club, a member died so Boyd went to his funeral. He was astonished and amused to see his school tie being worn by his old bunk mate now resting in his casket.

As for the Girls' Shack, it was a place where the young women of the day had a good deal of freedom. Many remember it as a camp experience – sleeping bags, no showers, one bathroom for the whole house, a place where teenagers could have fun on their own. Nan Carlin describes the Girls' Shack as "a kind of dump, clothes and sleeping bags strewn around, and the night watchman waking everyone as he clumped through in the middle of the night

Phyllis McLean (Firth) member from the Girls' Shack, with her mother, Lois McLean (Nancy Birks Hale Collection)

to stoke the furnace." (One of the Club's night watchmen was Bob, who also ran the old Dodge for Alex Foster's tow.)

Virginia and Nancy Birks
(Priscilla Penfield Chester Collection)

Although the Boys' and Girls' Shacks didn't change much, the Fifties would bring other innovations to the Shawbridge Club. Some members were still using the same skis for downhill and cross-country. There was a metal cable that fitted snugly into the groove that was around the heel of the boot. Sue Birks Dwyer describes how it worked: "For downhill skiing, we would snick the cables under some little hooks on the sides of the skis behind the instep; and for 'cross-country', we'd release them so our heels could lift up and down. They were convertible."

Naturally there were accidents. Banty Reid thinks that "Eileen Russel was probably responsible for the toboggan that always remained on the west verandah. Seems Eileen broke her leg on the trail and it was a problem to get her back until someone found an old outhouse door on which she could be carried or dragged without too much pain."

Considering the length of cross-country trips in those times, it is remarkable there weren't more accidents. An article in *The Canadian Ski Annual* describes a run from Labelle to Shawbridge, the day's distance being twenty-six miles covered in just under seven hours, "We reached the Laurentian Lodge at Shawbridge by 3:45 where after a shower, a glass of ale and a ham sandwich, the skiers were restored to a normal outlook on life."

During the post-war period into the Fifties, Mike Drummond writes that the Laurentians were more colourful than ever. "You'd take off from the Club and go for a quick ski at Lac-Archambault, and there'd be a bus arriving with all these characters half-pissed getting out, and the girls in their smart white leather ski-boots with white fur around the top, and a big sign on the bus, 'Immaculate Conception Ski Club'.

"On the hill I'd see these guys coming straight down because they didn't know how to turn, passing me at break-neck speed with four or five yards of different colours streaming on a string behind them, attached to the loop in their poles. It turned out to be a stream of tow tickets, a sort of prestige fad at that time."

In the Fifties, too, Club members were still skiing on the Big Hill although its days were numbered because of the planned Laurentian Autoroute. Hugh Seybold remembers one of the last races on the Big Hill: "When we got to the bottom, Mr. Harding had organized a table and there was George Trim serving 'French 75s', a combination of champagne and Guinness Stout, named after a famous World War One artillery gun. Of course we had several."

Spring skiing – when the snow was granulated like white sugar, the sun was warm and the sap was running – continued to be popular. Gerry Allen recalls the sugaring-off party, now a

Sugaring off, April 1959 (Nemec Family Collection)

Club tradition: "We'd go up to the station road to the farmer's sugar bush, usually skiing in from the road in the warm sunshine. There were horse-drawn sleighs and a shed with the boiling sap in full operation. Harry Lawton would bring up a small stove so eggs could be cooked in boiling sap!" When she got back to the Club, Gerry also remembers "getting into a game of Scrabble with Dr. Ted Rasmussen, Dr. Penfield's successor – big mistake as he used medical terms for three letter words."

On June 14, 1955, the Shawbridge Club was host to the Sedbergh School Old Boys who gave the "Chief" a surprise party for his eightieth birthday. Still skiing strongly, three years later he moved to a cabin surrounded by trees near Piedmont where he continued to lay out competitions, lead groups on cross-country ski trips, and returned often to the Club for his meals.

But something was about to occur that would change skiing customs at the Club and, indeed, throughout the entire Laurentians. Even as late as the Fifties, winter transportation by

"Jackrabbit" starting a race at the Sedbergh school (Hugh Wallis Collection)

car in the Laurentians could be an ordeal. "I remember in those years after World War Two," explains Hugh Seybold, a member of the Club's board of directors in 1954, "farmers who owned property along the new Curé Labelle highway (route 117) would plough the section of the road near their house. They would plough around the hill and charge you fifty cents to drive or be towed by their team of horses up the steepest bit."

All that would change with the coming of the Laurentian Autoroute in 1959. The Big Hill, no longer recognizable, had seen its last Test Run. Partly because the Autoroute now made it easier for skiers to drive to the Laurentians, do their thing and drive back in one day, the Club was closed except for four-day weekends. And most recreational skiers now changed from dual bindings to clamped downhill fittings and heavy boots so they could ski the tows all day long.

The same year as the Autoroute came through, the Club pulled off a master-stroke. They had always tried to maintain a fine table under chefs, like Mr. Harding himself, Harry Lawton and their successors. In 1959, André Pelrine was engaged: "I started as chef at the Sword and Anchor Inn in Halifax, an exclusive hotel. Later the manager of Chanteclerc said to me, 'I want you to work for Canadian Pacific. How would you like to come to Chanteclerc?' I almost said no but I came and then worked at the Manoir Richelieu at Murray Bay. The chef wanted me to go to Mexico, but I came back here. The first year I came to the Club I remember Les Perry sketching the little church down the road in the snow.

Eleanor Algie and Chef André Pelrine (L.L.C. Collection)

"Some of the members used to take part in those big championship races. I heard that one time, Harry Pangman missed the last train north. His race was the next morning. He set off on skis from Piedmont, skied through the night, went through the ice at least once, got wet and had to dry out. When he got to Tremblant, his race was just over."

Fortunately, André did not go to Mexico. He is still at the Club, smiling and gracious, coming out in his chef's hat after another delicious repast to accept the applause, still dishing up meals that would more than pass muster in a three-star Montreal restaurant and doing so for nigh on forty years. André in his kitchen means all's right with the Club.

THE SWINGING SIXTIES

At its convocation in 1960, McGill University bestowed an honorary degree on Club member, Senator A. Knatchbull-Hugessen. In his address, the Senator predicted that by the year 2010 McGill could expect a student population of 15,000 to 20,000, a prospect he called "monstrous".

The changes and unrest building in the Sixties, culminating in the assassinations of Martin Luther King and Bobby Kennedy, found little resonance at the Shawbridge Club where the beds were as lumpy and the dress codes as meticulous as they had been nearly fifty years before. It is remarkable that former members who have not been at the Club for half a century will still find the strings hanging from the bedroom lights, the three peep-holes for ventilation at the bottom of the windows, the famous brown bread on the dining room tables.

They could all relate to this description by Susan Craig, a member with her parents in the Sixties:

"If you slept in the big house there would be a symphony of sounds, the creaks and groans of the floors and the stairs, the night watchman clumping around after midnight, the mixed aroma of bacon and kippers and the silvery clatter of forks and knives as the kitchen came alive in the morning, the music and singing in the warm lounge in the evening. The Club was a welcoming place. It was amazing it was able to make all those different age groups feel at home."

Four Generations: Peggy Johannsen Austin; "Jackrabbit" (aged 107); Michael O'Gorman; and Karin Austin O'Gorman at the Canadian Marathon (Karin Austin O'Gorman Collection)

Much was heard in the Sixties about the generation gap. A reporter who interviewed "Jackrabbit" touched on this: "Johannsen has found the secret that makes the 'generation gap' a worthless phrase. He had discovered the living spark of adventure and purpose and friendship that many start out with, but later lose somewhere along the road of life."

In 1967, Centennial year, "Jackrabbit" at the age of ninety-two gave his enthusiastic support to the first annual Canadian Ski Marathon to run from Pointe Claire to Ottawa, a distance of 190 kilometres over three days and two nights. Members of the Shawbridge Club frequently participate in this classic Canadian event which continues to this day.

The Club itself, because of its many talented musicians and amateur thespians, encouraged what Susan Craig called "a symphony of sounds". Pat Irwin and Mike McBean were members of the Fossils, a well-known musical troupe in the West Island. Some of the Island City Singers were members of the Club. Don MacSween, a guest at the Club, and Jim Hugessen, an active member, were both involved in the enormously successful McGill revue, "My Fur Lady". Sing-songs around the piano Saturday evening were a must, led by Don Baillie on the violin and Gerry Allen, Bev Baily and others on the piano.

There was a novel piece of entertainment just before dinner one evening. Michael Drummond was there: "One night at the cocktail hour, the members were astounded to see one of the young waiters roller-skating into the living room, dressed in a little white coat with a black bow-tie and black trousers, balancing a silver tray of smoked salmon in one hand. Apparently the Club had been developing a problem. People were partying in their rooms with their own liquor and the bar revenues were way down. Harding, the manager, was not stupid so he provided a show. People were too embarrassed to bring their own liquor downstairs so for the next two or three years the bar thrived. Harding was a pro."

"Lost Again!" Dr. Margaret Mair and Joan Cleather

(L.L.C. Collection)

Numbers remained largely stable at the Club even when skiing trends were changing. Bill Ball writes in *I Skied the Thirties* that "it took cross-country skiing forty years to recover from the ski lift" rigged up by Alex Foster on the Big Hill in 1932 (sic). Of course more members of the Club took up downhill going to St-Sauveur, Gabriel, Avila and as far afield as Tremblant. But not that many gave up on cross-country. Somewhat but not altogether typical, is Banty Reid. Last winter at the age of ninety-one, Banty (who buys his downhill pass in September) skied at St-Sauveur in the morning, had a beer before the fireplace followed by lunch, then did cross-country for another hour or so.

Fortunately for the Shawbridge Club, by the early Seventies the pendulum had swung back to cross-country again. Joan Cleather, an administrator at McGill (women obtained full membership at the Club in 1964), explains why she and her husband Ted, a stockbroker, joined:

"In our case, it was partly the relief of not having to fight the tow lines or listen to the inane music at the foot of the hill, and partly the joy of crisp bright days in the woods and the adventure of setting out for the unknown." And there were the comforting rituals maintained by the Club like "waking early on a cold, frosty morning and, while still half asleep and buried under the covers, hearing the friendly morning sounds in the kitchen below. The stomping of boots to shake off the snow, the sounds and the pungent aromas of breakfast being prepared, transported me back to an earlier time at my grandmother's house when, as a child, I was free of all responsibilities and completely cared for."

"Off at last" (l. to r.) Ted Cleather, Joan Rothman, Susan Pahl and Joan Cleather (L.L.C. Collection)

After breakfast, Joan Cleather remembers "the front hall was bedlam; people rummaging for lost boots and jackets, others calling from the dining room that it wasn't worth skiing in pouring rain even if we dressed in green garbage bags, others emerging with questions about the best wax to use in a January thaw and everyone complaining about the weekend. Children were ducking under adult elbows on their way into the television room and Ted and I with our backs pressed back against the bulging coat-rack gawked in amazement at the chaos flowing around us.

"Suddenly, the front door opened and we heard a cheery voice pipe up as Gerry Allen stepped in from the porch, 'Well, at least it's stopped raining,' she said, and I thought to myself, I'm in the middle of an English farce; it's like a Noel Coward play ...

"When we finally got off, most of our excursions were three to four hour outings, marked by the inevitable bickering and second-guessing our leaders about the trails. With maps pulled out of packsacks and fingers freezing, we argued the best route. Sometimes, the long morning ski treks stretched into early afternoon and, although lunch was officially over, André would leave us a pot of thick soup, bean, vegetable or lobster bisque, simmering on the stove."

(r. to l.) Gerry Allen, her daughter, Peggy (Bagshaw) and Binnie Fairbanks (Club president, 1964) at Mont Gabriel, 1963

(L.L.C. Collection)

After the day's skiing, Heather Sargent, a teen at the time, describes returning "each evening to a cold shower, a warm fire, a soft drink and some snacks from the bar. The rooms were quaint and cozy, and we grew to love the dorm. As kids, we had supper as a gang before the adults and then retreated to the Games-TV room to hang out for a while, watching TV and playing 'pong'. As we grew older we would jump in someone's car and head out to a bar somewhere sneaking in as quietly as we could at a late hour."

Some adults weren't so lucky with their late night escapades. Two gentlemen friends, Bev Baily and Les Perry, not interested in bridge, reading, jig-saw puzzles, Scrabble or chit-chat, having been fortified against a cold January night by pre-dinner martinis and wine with their repast, "felt we should investigate a 'topless bar' we'd seen earlier in the day while returning from a ski at Tremblant." On their return the night clubbers found themselves locked out so they were forced to climb the fire escape. To their horror a welcoming committee of members was waiting to greet them, including Les Perry's wife, who was not amused. To add insult to injury, the nightclub was a bust: "The waitresses and dancers were swathed in heavy sweaters as the temperature outside was twenty-five degrees C. below and not much warmer in the bar."

So did the Shawbridge Club, in a minor way, participate in the climate of the Sixties and early Seventies, the era of dope smoking, hippies, the Civil Rights movement and the Summer of Love.

Banty Reid and Bev Baily at Mont Tremblant

(L.L.C. Collection)

THE MONASTERY

Le P'tit Train du Nord (CPR Collection)

So this was the Shawbridge Club – a medley of irreverence and formality, tumult and tradition, lounge lizards and zealous skiers – that my wife Catharine and I happily discovered in February, 1974. We had moved to Montreal from Toronto in the fall of 1972 (turning the key in the lock just as Paul Henderson scored his immortal goal against the Soviets) when I became Director of Public Affairs at radio station CJAD. Neither of us had ever done much skiing. My only experience was barrelling down a modest hill near Orangeville, Ontario, wildly gathering speed and in a fit of holy terror straddling the nearest tree in order to stop.

We didn't own a car when we arrived in Montreal so most weekends we crawled into our twenty-first floor apartment near the old Forum (Catharine was convinced our apartment building was run by the Mafia) and read all the newspapers including the Sunday *New York Times*. This was a recipe for depression, if not disaster. Or we would bundle up, venture out into the winter gales howling along Sherbrooke Street, and see how far we could go on a bus ticket (pretty well around the island if the drivers didn't look at the transfers). But we soon lost our zest for these expeditions as Catharine notes, "One blustery January day, as I shivered at the bus stop on Sherbrooke street near the Botanical Gardens, I decided we had to join the winter or perish from its cold."

So we began to explore. Catharine would make bus trips to the Laurentians scouting out possibilities because we needed a place where we could stay overnight. One day I was speaking with Mac McCurdy, station manager at CJAD (and a distant relative of J.A.D. McCurdy of *Silver Dart* fame). Mac asked if I had ever heard of the Shawbridge Club. I hadn't, so he put us in touch with Nancy Dawson, a long-time member.

The following Friday we bused up to the Laurentians and stayed overnight at a small motel on the outskirts of Piedmont (the village where "Jackrabbit" was living) and after breakfast Saturday morning we took a taxi to the Club, a solid two-storey building half-hidden by piled-up snow banks, dotted with skis, at the end of a short drive lined by evergreens on Shawbridge's Rue Principale.

I'll never forget the scene as we stepped from the cold sunny morning through the front door into the hallway teeming with skiers in various stages of undress, yelling for missing boots and mittens, arguing about which wax to use and trying to sort out who was going with whom and where. I recall noticing a handsome woman gaily waving around a cigarette. Turns out she was Madeleine O'Donnell, Prime Minister Louis St-Laurent's daughter.

Waiting for the "All Out!" (Heather Sargent Collection)

It didn't take Catharine and me long to decide, bedlam and all, this was the place for us. We applied for membership through Nancy Dawson, were accepted and invested in a cross-country package at Arlington's Sports shop – skis, poles and boots all for the princely sum of $49.99.

The next weekend almost ended in disaster for Catharine. She took the bus to Shawbridge:

"I started walking down the Station road to the Club when I saw Marjorie Reid and Nancy Dawson coming out to meet me. They took one look at my ski clothes and the little terry-cloth bag I was carrying (I was quite unaware of the dress code for dinner), then whisked me up the stairs to Nancy's room. Next thing I knew Dorothy Thompson was handing me one of her gorgeous silk blouses, Marjorie produced an elegant long wool skirt, and Margaret Mair, a popular pediatrician, arrived with high-heeled shoes and a pair of earrings, all accompanied by gales of laughter, the kind you'd hear in a girls' dorm in college. There was no looking back from that moment. The Club became our weekend home."

Both of us learned a lot about skiing from eighty-year-old Allan Turner Bone, who recovered from crippling arthritis by perseveringly skiing, pushing one foot after the other, when he couldn't walk. Allan was one of those skiers who, like the long gone Algonquins, preferred to stop frequently, look at the animal tracks, listen to the birds, and stand in the trail in a pool of sunlight and peel a juicy orange. Allan was a good teacher about skiing and about life.

To our amazement, a year or so ago the Club presented Catharine and me with a certificate noting we had now been members for a quarter of a century. During those years we had skied most of the regular trails – the Waterfall, the Barking Dog and the Patriarch among others. But one of our favourite outings lay north of St-Jovite where on the way I never failed to point out the white house with the red cross, a "monastery" housing self-styled nuns and brothers whose appointed "Pope" once sued me (unsuccessfully) for $100,000 when on a CJAD editorial I called him a "crook" after he had been convicted of kidnapping children.

Allan Turner Bone with "The Chief", 1976 (L.L.C. Collection)

We would leave the Club shortly after nine on a Saturday morning, drive an hour and a bit up the Autoroute, then highway 117, past St-Jovite and Gray Rocks and the old Hotel Bellevue, and thence into the grounds of the St-Bernard Monastery domain. This was a winter wonderland, home to a group of retired religious brothers, many of whom had spent their lives teaching in the French Roman Catholic schools in east-end Montreal and now lived in a rambling white wooden building with red-trimmed gables and a steep red roof.

We often saw the brothers out on their snowmobiles cleaning the ski trails (seventeen of them) that criss-crossed their property in Mont-Tremblant Park, the Devil's River gushing below one trail and in the spring, maple syrup boiling in vats along another. We never skied at the Monastery without stopping at a dépanneur to buy some seeds for the birds skittering around their numerous feeding stations along the wide Number One trail which encircled the mountain in the centre like a broad white scarf.

Indeed there was a special quality to skiing at the monastery as one stopped in a sunlit stand of pine, snow dropping from the evergreens like tinsel, then held out a handful of seeds for the birds who darted down, perched on your fingers and pecked away, then made way for others as though they had their own etiquette for eating. The birds, the water beneath the dark ice and the breeze in the snowy trees lent a spiritual quality to the scene, an awareness of being one with nature reminiscent of the early Algonquins – obeying nature's laws, smelling the flowers, drinking clear water, enjoying pure air and revelling in the songs of many birds, all blessings of the Manitou.

Near the Monastery (CPR Collection)

The Monastery had its own lively history. One day after a two-hour ski with our friends, Walter and Eleanor Lee, my wife remembers Walter taking us back to the Monastery house to meet some of the Frères St-Bernard and to decipher old documents. Walter's grandfather, Walter

Linus Lee, had made his living out of coal and he had once owned the whole mountain and the farm property at its base with its barns and outbuildings set in a European style square.

Walter also told us about his aunt, Ethel Lee, who managed the farm and a guest house in the Thirties: "Ethel Lee was a big woman who used a horse whip to advantage. She drove a team of fast horses, kept thirteen hunting dogs and always carried a gun in her carriage for shooting partridge." And there were other stories of the Monastery, some credible, some less so. Frank Nemec tells of the day he was skiing along the Monastery trails when he saw a religious brother getting off his ski-doo and heading deep into the woods. Frank was curious. Trained as he was in the Czech underground, he had no difficulty staying out of sight as he followed the brother's tracks. Suddenly the brother stopped at a large dead tree trunk, reached up, pulled out a bottle of whiskey and took a long swig. After he left, Frank crept up to the trunk, took out his own flask and filled the bottle to the top. Later in the day, Frank saw the brother return to the tree trunk, then heard him exclaim, "C'est un miracle!"

Nineteen seventy-five began with a gala party at the Shawbridge Club to mark "Jackrabbit's" hundredth birthday. It was hosted by the New England Ski Touring Council who showed up thirty strong to celebrate what "The Chief" had done to encourage cross-country skiing in the eastern United States when he lived at Lake Placid. His daughter, Alice, describes the scene: "There was an enthusiastic round of speeches, and a huge birthday cake, followed by a mass visit by the entire troop to his home in Piedmont to see where, almost fifty years later, he had put down his roots."

On March 9, the C.P.R. laid on "Le Jackrabbit Train de Ski", a revival of the old ski trains of the Thirties and Forties. This time though it was a six-car double-decker diesel train from the Windsor Station to Val-David. The mayor of Shawbridge drove "The Chief" to the Shawbridge

"Le Jackrabbit Train de Ski" arriving at Val-David, March 9, 1975, to celebrate "The Chief's" hundredth birthday. (Photo Don Lewis, Peggy Johannsen Austin Collection)

station in a horse and cutter where he joined hundreds of skiers (with a good contingent from the Shawbridge Club), dressed in colourful garb, as they all settled in the coaches with ukeleles and accordions singing the ski songs of the old days.

It was a time of tributes from all sides, many collected by Brian Powell in his excellent book, *Jackrabbit: His First Hundred Years.* Thomas D. Cabot of the noted Boston family goes back to the Twenties:

"This strong, wiry man with the profile of an eagle..." Wilder Penfield
(Photo Michael Drummond)

"In the early 1920s, several of us from Boston who thought we knew how to ski joined the Laurentian Lodge Club, organized by skiers from Montreal at Shawbridge, Quebec. There we met Herman Smith Johannsen. All of us were in awe of the grace and speed that Jackrabbit displayed on his narrow birch skis, and we were always delighted when we could have a skoal or a game of 'Cardinal's Puff' with him at the clubhouse."

A fellow member, Wilder Penfield, wrote his own tribute for "The Chief's" hundredth birthday: "This strong, wiry man with the profile of an eagle, Johannsen, is the Pied Piper, one might say, of the ski hills. He called in his clear, high voice and the young and the strong came flocking after him to discover the cold, white beauty of the North."

It was about the time of his birthday that my wife and I would encounter "The Chief" when he came over to the Club from his cabin at Piedmont for lunch. Still lean and wiry, his Nordic face tanned by the sun, he waddled rather than walked, extra careful of the balance that helped him "bushwhack" down Tremblant, catching at tree branches to steady his descent. Naturally, he was asked how he accounted for his longevity. His answer went something like this: "I believe in smoking my pipe – but only one pipe a day. And having a small drink and enjoying it – but only one a day. You see, knowing when to stop, that's the secret."

One day shortly after an early lunch, I ran into the "Chief" in the lounge. He was sitting contemplatively in the corner beside the fire smoking a cigarette. He waved the cigarette toward the flames and said to me somewhat mischievously, "I never smoke one of these before lunch but I often have lunch early." Sometimes he would begin dinner at the Club by saying grace in Cree.

During these years, too, the Club remained blessed with its staff. The first manager, the popular Leigh Harding, had left in 1959 because of ill health and was replaced in turn by the Eastwoods, the Gosselins and finally, in 1977 by John Schwab, a sailor with the Royal St. Lawrence Yacht Club and a skier who did much for younger skiers – founding the Ski Hawk Clubs and the Ravens. Bev Baily said hiring John Schwab was the best move he made during his presidency.

John Schwab with the "Chief", 1983 (Photo Michael Drummond)

John Schwab, the strong planes of his features reminiscent of John Wayne, had the healthy outdoor look of a man who spent time in the wind, on the sea and the ski slopes. John had that rare ability to mix sociably yet retain his authority to manage the Club's business with fairness and courtesy. During the war he trained pilots in emergency procedures. Gary Selby, a night watchman says, "John Schwab had a magic touch with people. His style was laid back with a deep respect for others."

There was, however, one area where John's views were suspect – his weather reports. Whenever you telephoned from Montreal to inquire about snow conditions, John would invariably reply, "Great, come on up," even if all the snow had turned to frozen slush. But John had one thing right. One should never look at the bare streets of Montreal (or give too much credence to the weather reports) and conclude snow conditions up north were hopeless. Many a time I remember returning to Montreal after a weekend of great skiing, only to be met with the incredulous and predictable response from a neighbour, "But look at the streets, there's no snow."

May Buick Selby is another staff member whose quiet friendly way makes the Club so welcoming. May, a distance relative of the famous Buick car family ("My father's cousin, a Buick, sold all his shares in the company, invested his money in something else and died broke"), first started working at the Club in 1957:

"Harry Lawton was like a second father to me. When I first came to work at the Club, he gave me the uniform to wear. That uniform was grey cloth with a white apron over it, and white cuffs and collar, with a cap, all starched and stiff. I thought I looked like the people you see in a prison uniform; all the waitresses wore them until Mr. Schwab stopped all that when he became manager."

Joan Cleather describes John Schwab as "genial and unflappable," which is about right. Joan also writes about one of the Club's most popular members, Eleanor Algie as "the elegant

"Lady Eleanor" pouring tea for Libby Leslie and Charlie Harris (L.L.C. Collection)

ageless matrix of the Club". Eleanor Algie joined the Shawbridge Club in 1979 when she was 71. Now in the year 2000, she is one of the first to arrive from Montreal on Friday for lunch and the last to leave Sunday afternoon, driving her own car and skiing most days. She's given up the "Valley of the Fallen Women" and now sticks pretty much to the train tracks beside the North River below where the Big Hill used to be before the Autoroute came through.

Eleanor, (referred to by Ted Cleather as "Lady Eleanor") is in her element presiding over "High Tea" in the lounge (scones, honey and blueberry jam, clotted cream, dainty sandwiches) pouring piping hot Earl Grey tea from silver teapots in her floor-length maroon gown, long white gloves and colourful shawl setting off her snowy white hair.

The dining room was extended during Banty Reid's presidency in 1969 "because the Club was getting too crowded and noisy around dinner time with all the young people playing musical instruments just outside the doorway." This made the dining experience at the Club that much more special. André consistently turns out superb meals from the Club's antiquated kitchen. His roast beef, rare and swimming in savoury juices, preceded by a tangy shrimp cocktail or a creamy lobster bisque and followed by a homemade chocolate cream pie, constitutes the first part of the evening. Then the president calls on volunteers for after-dinner stories, some hoary, others on the cusp of the risqué, followed at times by a sing-song around the piano, more often by reading beside the fire, conversation or a table of bridge.

Chef André Pelrine and May Buick (L.L.C. Collection)

It was in the Seventies too that the Club applied for and received a grant from the federal New Horizons program to help seniors with various activities. Naturally, the Club applied for, among other things, money to purchase new beds, the current ones not all that much better than those bought from the Montreal General Hospital for three dollars each almost sixty years earlier. However, the federal ministry turned down the request for beds: "I guess," snapped Betty Meek, "they don't believe in indoor sports."

THE DEATH OF A LEGEND

For most of the Seventies, Catharine and I usually caught "Le P'tit train du Nord" (the C.P.R. had revived it) every Friday evening at Westmount Station. There were many skiers aboard, some plucking away at banjos, some sitting, others just staring through the frosty windows relishing the deepening snow as we got beyond St-Jérôme. Once the snow was so deep and the temperature so low that the train screeched, slowed, then stopped altogether, the tracks too frozen and slippery for the wheels to obtain traction.

But most times we arrived at the Shawbridge station on time, about seven-thirty. If no one met us, we would walk the fifteen minutes to the Club in the bracing cold, past houses twinkling with holiday lights, white plumes of smoke lazily curling from the chimneys, and the snappy crunch of snow underfoot, until we saw the warm lights of the Club at the end of the tree-lined driveway off Rue Principale .

John Schwab, who sometimes met us at the station, would always have a piping hot dinner ready (thanks to André), and we would eat on trays beside the fireplace in the cozy lounge. There was something special about Friday evenings at the Club. For one thing there were fewer people, before the boisterous crowds bustled in early Saturday morning. This gave the evening a quiet intimacy, a feeling of family, as the members sat around the lounge after dinner, reading, playing bridge or just talking in little groups.

Joan Fitzpatrick and Lois Pangman in the lounge

(L.L.C. Collection)

It was during those tranquil evenings that Catharine and I got to know and appreciate people like Lois and Harry Pangman. The Pangmans were a serene couple who radiated an inner strength. Lois sat quietly knitting, occasionally going over to check the unreliable thermostat on those nights the frost was as thick as a coat of paint on the windows. Harry, in his plaid shirt, blue corduroy pants and red socks was one of those rare men who is comfortable with silence. Sometimes, though, he would reminisce about his old skiing days, the first trip up Tremblant in 1930, winning the first Kandahar race, the 1932 Olympics, helping to found the Red Birds and most often about his good friend and skiing companion, Herman Johannsen. I remember one Friday night he talked about "bushwhacking":

"You know, Herman almost invented the name 'bushwhacking'. It came from his habit of swinging from one tree-branch to the next to break his descent. After the starter's gun went off in a 'bushwhacking' race, you were on your own and everything went. Forget the rules. And use whatever helped – special sticks for pole riding, crash helmets, elbow guards, skis wrapped in burlap, you name it, if it helped, we used it. The whole thing was to get down the hill as straight and as fast as you could and, if possible, in one piece."

So as we sat in the lounge talking about the old days and about where we might ski on the morrow, the warmth of the fire blended into the warmth of friendship as the Club worked its magic. There was the feeling of being connected and content, a feeling that it was good to be here with friends.

Dorothy Thompson on a Club trail with family, 1950

(Linda Thompson Sinclair Collection)

Sometimes too in the mid-Seventies, before we got our own car, we would drive to the Club on Friday afternoon with Dorothy Thompson, a refined lady, always fashionably dressed for dinner "in her long skirts and fancy blouses", as her daughter, Linda, who joined the Club with her parents in the Fifties, remembers. Once a year Dorothy would invite her son-in-law, Gord Sinclair, News Director at Montreal radio station CJAD, to come up with Linda for dinner. Gord, a good friend of mine, recalls listening to "Jackrabbit" saying a few words on the occasion of his 106th birthday: "He never spoke in the past tense or the present tense, only in the future tense."

In 1981, the Club newsletter, written by John Schwab, noted that membership was limited to ninety (there are twenty-one double bedrooms) and the Club was full up most weekends so that on Saturday night children slept with their parents or in the bunk rooms. On New Year's Eve that year there were fifty adults and twenty-five children swinging and swaying to Bob Hill's music. But in less than a decade this picture would change dramatically. In 1989 there were fewer adults for New Year's and only four younger people.

What were the reasons for this decline? Of course, the widespread use of the automobile gave families more options. On New Year's Eve, for example, many still came for André's dinner and Heather Thompson's entertainment, then drove back to Montreal at ten o'clock.

There were other reasons for this drop-off in membership. What appealed to younger people in the old days when, for example, the Dodge family had four generations at the Club (as did the Johannsens), no longer had the same allure. With a wide variety of other entertainment available – from the Grateful Dead to rave parties – younger people had little interest dancing the Gay Gordons to musical records (Bob Hills' orchestra had now become too expensive).

Dr. Bill Fisher and André escorting the haggis on Robbie Burns' night
(L.L.C. Collection)

John Schwab, in his inimitable manner, noted this decline in his newsletter at the end of the 1990 season: "To ensure the Club's future, the present membership should start having children or introduce some younger families who already have them." With rare exceptions this did not happen. Instead the adult membership also dwindled. This was the trend at the time in most family clubs in Quebec and the Shawbridge Club was no exception. Some families left the province. Others rented or built their own places in the Laurentians or the Eastern Townships when their children grew older. And if their children skied at all, they chose Alpine. Cross-country was too boring.

This decline was masked, to some degree, by those members and their guests who still came to the Club but only for special occasions. One of the most popular was Robbie Burns night when the haggis was piped into the lounge by a piper in full Black Watch regalia and after a blessing, a round of toasts and a splendid dinner, Dr. Bill Fisher would recite some of Burns' poems in the Scots dialect. St. Patrick's night became equally popular with shamrocks on the table, crème de mênthe for dessert, dissertations in Gaelic by Dr. Gus O'Gorman and a toe-

Jill Pangman and her father win the darts' trophy on Pub Night.
(L.L.C. Collection)

Aisling and Michael O'Gorman on St. Patrick's night

(L.L.C. Collection)

tapping display of Irish dancing by two of "Jackrabbit's" great-grandchildren, Aisling and Michael O'Gorman, cheered on by their parents, Gus and Karin, clapping as hard as everyone else.

Pub night featured bangers and mash and a hard-fought darts competition where those who hit the wall or the ceiling were hailed just as loudly as those who pierced the bull's-eye. On Tyrolean nights we put feathers in our hats and skied on the golf course waving torches that lit up the darkness like a necklace of phosphorescent pearls and on the night featuring André's gourmet buffet, we just sat down and relished the food. Recently John Hallward introduced a wine-tasting party that has proved popular.

But the popularity of these events illustrated another worrisome trend. Increasingly, some members were now using the Club as a social venue rather than a place to ski. Like the chaps in *The New Yorker*, some found it more inviting to sit down to a sumptuous dinner than to ski down the slopes. This downward drift (exacerbated by rental squabbles with the golf club) continued through the Nineties when the Club's board and the membership at large began to explore remedies. An obvious one is to attract more younger members through promoting the simplicity, the relatively low cost and the environmental friendliness of the Club.

An effort is also going forward to advertise the Club's facilities for the use of outside groups such as colleges and universities organizing workshops and seminars. Professor Jim Moore, of Concordia, has, with good results, been informing the academic community of the Club's facilities. The Liberal Arts College at Concordia now holds its annual Medieval Days weekend at the Club. Dr. Gus O'Gorman organized another weekend for the study of Gaelic. Social events such as wedding receptions, birthdays and anniversaries, have also been held at the Club. The current board is convinced that exploring imaginative new uses for the Club will secure its financial viability aided by the creative accounting practices of treasurer, Kenny Farmer. Sadly, these efforts will miss the input of John Schwab. After nearly a quarter of a century of dedicated service, the Club's popular manager has retired with the good wishes of all the members.

Other things never change at the Club – discussing ski waxes, hors d'oeuvres and drinks before dinner in the lounge and the excellence of Chef André's cuisine. "The best part of staying at the Club," writes Louise Spalding, "was the food. No fancy diet for André. His soups were to die for and his porridge could sustain you all day." Dining customs were religiously maintained by John Schwab. "We have been asked to remind the gentlemen members that jackets are to be be worn in the evenings for dinner (a turtle neck rather than a tie will do)."

Then again, a few things did change. In 1983, Norma Rollit, an extremely capable businesswoman, became the Club's first woman president. Her husband Tubby, with his big waist, big laugh and big cigar, once became so enraged at the season's supply of wet wood, hissing and spitting in the fireplace, that he stormed out and promptly bought several loads of the best dry wood he could find.

The fire was at the centre of another of those many circles of common bonds at the Club – the self-appointed fire persons. Ever so often one of us would peer knowingly at the fire the way a surgeon peers at an x-ray and, depending on our prognosis, we would give the fire a kick, or fan it with the bellows, or if we judged it was *in extemis,* we would tear it all down and start again with rolls of newspapers. (John Schwab had the annoying habit of burning the Saturday papers on Saturday, especially disgusting for those of us who got up early to venture out on a bone-chilling morning to buy them.) The most respected fire persons were those elite few who, eschewing matches and lighters, could ignite the morning fire just using the smouldering coals from the night before.

Norma Rollit, the Club's first woman president with Eleanor Algie (L.L.C. Collection)

The glowing fireplace attracted members for different reasons. The meditative types, balancing a cup of coffee on their laps, just stared at the fiery coals, as if mesmerized; others kicked the fire whenever they passed; still others pulled their chair as close as possible and settled in with a magazine, a book or *The New York Times'* crossword puzzle and some just gave themselves over to the somnolent warmth and snoozed.

Once after an especially heavy lunch (the hamburger diet plate has more calories than a porterhouse steak) Kenny Farmer, of McGill hockey fame, was quietly snoring away. Suddenly Joan Fitzpatrick, tapping away on her laptop, "spotted a plume of smoke rising from the toe of Ken's slipper. A spark had jumped from the fire and started to burn in the warmth of the slipper's fleece." A startled Kenny Farmer awoke to find fellow-snoozers whacking away at his foot.

It was about this time that fire took on a more serious aspect at the Club. Inspectors from the Régie came around sniffing at everything from the furnace in the basement to the smoke detectors upstairs. Then they packed their briefcases and went away. Several weeks later they came back, all looking unhealthy and wearing suits, and mandated thirty-two changes to be made pronto in the Club's fire prevention system. The members, who were suspicious of all government watch dogs, reacted with a healthy dose of skepticism neatly captured by Joan Fitzpatrick, "The relief we felt when we were assured our bedroom doors would now take all of 45 minutes to burn through."

On January 5, 1987, the Club heard the sad news. Herman Smith Johannsen, the "Chief" had died of pneumonia while visiting his son, Bob, in his beloved Norway, where he had been

"Jackrabbit", aged 102, Eva Olsson of Sweden and Shirley Firth of Canada, at the North American Ski Championships (Peggy Johannsen Austin Collection)

"All my life I have been anxious to see what lies on the other side of the hill, and at the same time to enjoy the scenery along the way. Climb your mountain slowly, one step at a time. And when at last you stand upon the summit, you can look beyond, to the farthest horizon."

born 111 years before. Many members of the Club attended the memorial service at the Church of St. Francis in St-Sauveur, which Herman had attended and where he had been a warden. He was buried, as he had wished, beside Alice (who had died in 1963) in the village's little cemetery containing the striking granite boulder that bears their dates and names.

Many thousands of years ago during the continental ice age, the glaciers carried this boulder from its site somewhere in the Laurentians to Mont St-Hilaire where it was beached when the glacial ice melted. For many more thousands of years, lying on an abandoned ocean beach, the boulder was rounded and polished by the waves of the Champlain Sea, which had overrun the St. Lawrence Valley, making an island of Mont St-Hilaire.

And so the boulder symbolizes the connection with the misty origins when the land mass buckled, the oceans moved and out of this maelstrom the Laurentians first appeared, to be scraped and gouged by the glaciers, weighed down by the ice sheets, and emerge again when the ice retreated. Thus the granite boulder connects to this long history and to the human history of the Laurentians too. "Jackrabbit" always obeyed the laws of nature prescribed by the Council of the Manitou 1,500 years ago: "Do not kill except to defend yourself or by necessity; love even the most humble plant; respect the trees."

For almost sixty years "Jackrabbit" had been a member of the Shawbridge Club. From there he organized his first trip up Tremblant, from there he watched over the Test Runs, from there he taught his young friends to ski and it was there, over a drink and a pipe, he maintained his friendships with his older friends, Percy Douglas, Harry Pangman, Banty Reid and all the others.

"He was," Anne Murdoch sums up, "the glue that kept all the rest together from the early Thirties almost to his death."

Linked Music; the Wurtele sisters (Canadian Ski Museum)

LINKED MUSIC

Throughout the years, the Club followed the old traditions and developed new ones. In mid-November there was the trail clearing. A handful of enthusiastic members would gather to cut the growth on the various trails. Some would bring clippers, saws and axes, others rum and a pail in which to melt snow and boil water for tea.

At the end of November came the opening dinner, renewing friendships over hors d'œuvres and drinks in the lounge culminating in André's splendid meal followed by a masterpiece of quite a different order as Joan Fitzpatrick explains:

"The very first time I went to the opening dinner as a guest I couldn't believe what I was hearing. Ken Farmer, the treasurer [Ken became a senior partner at the accounting firm, Coopers and Lybrand], was giving his annual financial report. He started out by mentioning the national debt, the provincial debt and the Montreal Urban Community debt, and then said, in comparison, we were in pretty good shape. At this all the members laughed uproariously. They were more concerned about the first snow and who was going to be at the New Year's party.

"With a group such as this one whose priorities were definitely in the right order, the only solution left was to join them, which I did, and have been absolutely delighted with my membership ever since."

The opening dinner was followed by Christmas Ski Week and the New Year's Eve party.

Catharine and I usually drove up to the Club on Boxing Day in our own car. The party at New Year's became more elaborate with a series of skits put on by the members and produced with enthusiasm and skill by Heather Thompson. These gave an opportunity to relive disasters on the trails as well as lampoon politicians like Bill Clinton, Jean Chrétien and Lucien Bouchard. One of the most memorable for me was the occasion of my seventieth birthday and the subject was my new passion for golf. Dressed haphazardly in my own duds, Joan Fitzpatrick was swinging a menacing five-iron before addressing the ball when another golfer burst in from the wings yelling, "Stop, that's the ladies' tee." "Get out of my way," barked Joan, "this is my second shot." Heather Thompson's New Year's Revue always plays to enthusiastic standing-room-only audiences.

And the entertainment is followed by vigorous dancing. One of the dances involved tying a balloon to your ankle, then stomping as hard as you could to strike and explode the balloons of the other dancers. There were squeals, squawks and pops all over the dimly lit dance floor as you danced past the

Heather and Nigel Thompson reading scripts for New Year's Eve Revue (L.L.C. Collection)

The McKentys struggling with the balloon dance (L.L.C. Collection)

Bill Keating and Garnice Ware at the Club's spring cook-out (L.L.C. Collection)

fireplace and the gaily decorated Christmas tree, kicking all the while as hard and as often as you could. The last couple standing, the "survivors", were the winners. The balloon dance left you perspiring and thirsty, ready for something cold on the rocks, but it was almost as difficult to push through the animated crowd at the bar as it was to slalom down the "Chief's" trail at the edge of the golf course.

January and February were the months for real skiing, away from the icy winds howling through the canyon that is Sherbrooke Street, and onto the trails through the woods at the Patriarch and the Waterfall where the winter winds did not blow and chances are, whatever the temperature, you might need to shed a sweater. There were hardy groups that set off early Saturday morning and returned just in time for a late lunch about 2:30. Among the devotees of four- and five-hour trips were the Pahls, the Moores, Zib Fraser, Dr. Ian Hutchison, Gail Jarislowsky, the Jaques, Dr. Ann Macaulay, Betsy Mitchell, Frank Collins, sometimes the Brookers as well as others. Probably Bill Keating, a Westmount lawyer, should be in the group if only for the vast array of equipment he carried. Bill lugged around dried fruit, a whistle, a ship's compass, several heavy duty flares, cigars, and more recently a cell phone the better to contact Frank Nemec five miles away on the Patriarch to compare trail conditions.

My own favourite time for skiing was the spring, those sunny melting days of late February and March, gliding through the trees looking down on the Devil's River at the Monastery beyond St-Jovite. Sometimes you would stand still in a grove of trees and just listen to the sun-splashed water bubbling below, to the birds above your head, darting down and perching in your hand, bowing and bobbing like miniature priests as they bolted the corn seeds, listen to the snow, cotton balls on the evergreens, melting and falling with a gentle thump.

Paradoxically, these natural and familiar sounds, seem to heighten the enveloping silence. For me, this silence, deep in the snowy woods, carries a spiritual quality in the sense that it leads naturally to an awareness of a power greater than oneself, whether that power is a force of nature or a personal God.

One person who has written eloquently of skiing in this vein is the pioneer British skier, Sir Arnold Lunn, who skied with "Jackrabbit" Johannsen, Harry Pangman, Percy Douglas and other members of the Shawbridge Club. Sir Arnold is writing about Nordic skiing in the Alps but what he says applies also to the Laurentians:

"Between the ski-runner and the hillside there is nothing but an inch of sensitive ash, which responds to every change of rhythm of the slope. As the ski rise and fall, leaping over the hillocks and diving into the dips, they seem living and vital things with a will that is all their own. They borrow their motion, not from petrol or steam, but from the mother earth itself. In their simplicity they approach as near wings as anything we are likely to find this side of the grave ...

"The joy of skiing is not only physical but intellectual. The expert ski-runner is forced to study Nature in one of her most fascinating moods. He must adapt his tactics to every mood of the hills, to every fickle fancy of the snow ..."

Sir Arnold then describes a ski run down the mountain side and through the trees:

"Before you quite realize what has happened, you are off, and you hear music, whose echoes haunt you through the long summer months, the hiss of the snow as your ski drive through the crystals. A few curves and you decide to risk a straight run. The wind rises into a tempest and sucks the breath out of your body. A lonely fir swings past like a telegraph pole seen from an express train...

"You sweep out on to a gentle slope, and the hurricane dies away. You glory in the sense of control, which you have recaptured over your ski, no longer untamed demons hurrying you through space, but the most docile of slaves. You are playing with gravity; you are the master of the snow; you can make it yield like water and resist like steel ... But now the snow changes once again, and the breakable crust gives place to solid crust slightly softened in the sun, a glorious running surface. You run down in a series of stem christianias, long sweeping curves on the sure, straight surface.

"Now you have reached the forest line. You can choose between an open glade and a thousand feet of running through the trees ... Wood running is perhaps the most delightful of all forms of skiing ...

"The trees thin out into a thousand feet of open country ... You sweep down the powder snow

'In many a winding bout
Of linked music long drawn out'."

Linked Music (CPR Collection)

A MAGICAL PLACE

Sometimes an experience at the Club would change a life's direction. Denis Drummond, while still in the Boys' Shack, recalls starting out on his last Test Run:

"While stopping in deep snow, and without falling, I felt a sudden pain in the area of an old repaired fracture in my left leg. So I returned as quickly as I could to the Club. What other Club in the world could you consult with such medical giants, right in front of the fireplace, with a drink in hand?

"First on the scene was Wilder Penfield, the world's best known neurosurgeon at that time. He confessed fractures were not his area of expertise but confirmed the diagnosis. Moments later he deferred to another member, Jim Shannon, Chief of Orthopaedic Surgery at the Montreal General Hospital. He gave me a piece of his mind for the disruption of his earlier work on my leg, and arranged for admission to hospital for what turned out to be successful surgical repair.

"Dr. Shannon was a remarkable man – a role model who as much as anyone was responsible for my decision to pursue first medical school, then orthopaedic surgery and finally a career teaching my craft. At McGill Medical School, I was able to learn from both of my famous Shawbridge consultants. As I reflect on this, the test run accident turned out to be lucky. After all, it changed the direction of my life."

And sometimes, another kind of experience at the Club would shape a life in a different fashion. Rick Sargent, a Club president and his wife, Millie, a handsome dark-haired woman, were two of the Club's most popular members early in the Eighties. Then Millie was diagnosed with cancer. Her fellow members rallied round as best we could. I remember Millie, smiling and serene, seated among swirling dancers in the darkened lounge, her face wreathed in the light from the holiday decorations and the flames of the fire, presiding over her last New Year's party. Her daughter, Heather, remembers too:

"Auld Lang Syne around the fire at midnight at New Year's Eve was always an emotional time for me. It is where I remember spending the last few years with my mom before she died. It is where I saw my parents struggling silently with my mom's imminent death, and it is where I saw my father rebuild after she died. It is where I remember challenging him to a cross-country ski race after partying all night in the city. It is where I remember seeing my dad as a person who loved to go to Shawbridge as much or more than my sister and I did. It is where I saw him relax, and where I learned of having something in life to strive for, a place to get away together, a place to share. It is where I learned of a history that joined me to so many before me like Mr. Johannsen and those who came after, Jill Drummond and her brother, Peter, Trish Heward, Jeff Keating, the Tildens, the Mairs, and the list goes on and on.

"The Shawbridge Club is where I learned how simple a place can be that spans so long and so much in our hearts. It is where I grew up."

Jill Pangman also remembers her parents, Lois and Harry:

"Both my parents' approach to the outdoors and to the natural world was a gentle one. They trod on the earth gently and they gave me a love and passion for the outdoors. I think the reason they were so welcomed by all age groups in their community, Senneville, and also at the Club, was that they were both young at heart. They loved children, they loved to laugh and they kept physically active almost to the end of their lives.

"My parents never had a Laurentian getaway cottage; the Club became their getaway destination, a chance to spend many winter weekends in the country with good skiing just out the front door. And the Club brought them much joy in their later years and helped filled the gap left by the absence of family.

Harry Pangman doing what he loves

(Canadian Ski Museum Collection)

"My father taught me to not only enjoy skiing and many outdoor activities but also to love it, to have a passion for the outdoors which is, I suppose, why I got involved in conservation issues and wilderness guiding in the Yukon where I now live.

"I remember once asking Dad when I spent a month with him the winter before he died, if there was anything he would like to have done differently. He was quiet for a few moments. Then he looked at me and said, quite matter of factly, 'I wish I had skied more!' At the time I remember thinking, 'Is that all?' But when I thought more about his words, I realized they summed up much of his character. My father was not a person to harbour regrets. He lived for the moment and he tried his best to live the present moment to the full.

"Later at Tremblant, with family and friends, I placed a plaque honouring my father, high in the Laurentian Mountains, on the peak that bears his name. It is engraved with the words of a Sami herdsman: 'I would like to die as I have lived. Disappear among the tundra winds. Be transformed into birdsong.'

"My father was not only my friend but my mentor. At the Club and elsewhere he instilled in me a reverence for wild lands and my love for all that is untamed."

Others express what the Shawbridge Club means to them in other ways. "As soon as we got to the Club," writes Elizabeth Turner Bone MacEwan, "a magical world opened." Phyllis Dodge remembers the bells:

"The jingle of the bells on the horses' harnesses pulling the sleighs that brought us from the C.P.R. station; the rising bell; the thirsty man's bell at the bar and Harry Lawton's meal-time bell." And some of the other sounds: "the hissing of many showers, the gurgling of emptying bathtubs; the slap-slap of slippers on the linoleum floors; the tick-tock of ping-pong balls from the games' room and the frosty clunking sound of a Shawbridge Club Special being shaken in the bar."

"The whole thing at the Club," concludes Karin Austin O'Gorman ("Jackrabbit's" grandchild), "was keeping things simple. That eliminated people who wanted a phone in their

room or wall-to-wall carpeting. I suppose at one time the Club was quite ritzy but there are no waiters in white coats now serving drinks on the front lawn."

"We were young," recalls Douglas McEwan, "and the birch logs in the huge fireplace were warmer and smokier, the brown bread was richer, the laughter shook your whole body, the wooden floor boards creaked on the way to bed, and the lumpy beds were deeper and softer for the tingling tired muscles." "It was like a huge house party," says Jean Peters Dupont, "without any trouble about who would cater or whom to invite."

In the Sixties, Montreal Calendar called it "the ... private ski Club that counts some of the most legendary cross-country skiers in Quebec amongst its members." "We developed some fine skiers," wrote Percy Douglas, president of the Canadian Amateur Ski Association, and one of the Club's original members, "men and girls, all ages, and toured for miles over the lovely, rolling country that lies to the east and the west. The Club, under the management of the wonderful Harding family, has met with continuing success from the start, and membership is a high privilege."

In 1924, as a boy of ten, Gordon Shaw worked at the Club for Harry Lawton: "Nothing much has changed in the seventy-odd years since I first went there. The lounge with the fieldstone fireplace is as welcoming as ever. It always was a homey place where people relaxed." "And where," writes Eileen Russel, "our best memories are of the members we met and skied with and who became our friends."

Priscilla Penfield, whose famous father joined in 1930, calls the Club a "magical place". Early one day in March, 1949, she invited a young man from Harvard to the Club for lunch, then accompanied him for an afternoon's skiing on the Big Hill. This sparked a whirlwind romance, culminating a short time later when, on a trip back to Montreal from skiing at Gray Rocks, her young man, Bill Chester, pulled off the road, stopped the car, turned to Priscilla and proposed. They have now been married for more than half a century.

Other romances blossomed at the Club – George McTaggart won Lois Ibbotson's heart when he visited the Club, held her hand and told her fortune; Mary Leslie and Ian Aitken met on a trail-clearing party; Jim Hugessen, later a judge on the Federal Court in Ottawa, describes what happened to him:

"As a child, I was taught to play bridge (badly). We often played at the Club. One evening Herbie Lewis and I, both ten or eleven, took on two girls of our own age, Efa Heward and a rather chubby classmate of hers from The Study.

"The girls were guests of Efa's aunt, Mrs. Chil Heward. She was a great card shark and on this occasion she helped the girls to bid a grand slam, which Efa's partner made. To this day, I maintain that I was cheated and that Mrs. Heward had looked at all the hands and then told the girls what to do, both on bidding and playing the cards. The girl in question denies it and says the whole thing was above board. I have no recourse. Her name was Mary Stavert and we have been married for forty-one years."

Romance. Stories. Memories. So many memories. The soft rolling Laurentians, lovely in the light of a winter's evening, slowly receding into the mists of the Manitou; singing on the ski trains in the mellow light of the gas lanterns; waiting at the station for Maxwell and the Percherons, steaming in the frosty night, as they pull the welcoming sleigh with "Shawbridge Club" in bright red letters on the side; waiting at breakfast for "Jackrabbit" to appear with his cheery invitation, "Who's for skiing? All out!"

And that first ride on "Foster's Folly" desperately trying to keep your mitts from going through the pulley and being shredded like cornflakes; Mario, nonchalant in his dark goggles, glistening with suntan lotion; noses twitching from the acrid smell of waxes being rubbed on skis Saturday morning; and the sweet aroma of the brown bread, rich with molasses; squeaky floors and lumpy beds and the gala seventy-fifth anniversary party.

Skiing on the powdery snow at the Waterfall or stopping to peel a tangerine at the Monastery and watching the sun dancing on the Rivière-du-Diable before returning to the Club for a bath, a drink in front of the fireplace, and a bottle of wine with André's splendid repast.

Watching John Schwab pull the curtains against the dark and cold of a wintry night, staring at the glowing coals as the shadows lengthen in the lounge, and listening to a final story about the legends of the Club before its time to put out the lights and climb the squeaky stairs for bed.

So many legends. So many memories. So many friends through the years – seventy-seven years – tracing their tracks in the Laurentians snows. The Shawbridge Club. It was – and is – "a magical place".

SELECTED BIBLIOGRAPHY

Arbique, Louise (with Marc Blais). *Mont Tremblant: Following the Dream.*
Les Éditions Carte Blanche, Montréal, 1998.
This is a handsome and informative book containing colourful background about Laurentian pioneers.

Ball, William L. *I Skied the Thirties.*
Deneau Publishers and Company Ltd. Ottawa.
A good over-view of early skiing by one who did it.

Berton, Pierre. *Vimy.*
McClelland & Stewart. Toronto, 1986.
An exciting account of the great battle.

Canadian Ski Annuals, *passim.*

Chronicle of Canada. Montreal, 1990.
Good for checking events in the wider context.

Collard, Edgar Andrew. *All Our Yesterdays.*
The Gazette, Montreal,1988.
Always a pleasure to read on the early days.

Cornez, Germaine. *Une Ville Naquit:* Saint-Jérôme de 1821 à 1880.
Éditions l'Echo du Nord, Saint-Jérôme, 1973.
Excellent material on Curé Labelle.

Douglas, H. Percy. *My Ski-ing Years.*
Whitcombe & Gilmour Ltd., Montreal, 1951.
Excellent descriptions of early skiing.

Eber, Dorothy. *Genius at Work: Images of Alexander Graham Bell.*
McClelland and Stewart, 1982
A visually beautiful account of the Baddeck years.

Graham, Joe. *The Doncaster Letters* (unpublished).
Valuable detail on the history of Ste-Agathe region.

Grignon, Dr. Edmond. *Album-Historique de la Paroisse de Ste-Agathe-des-Monts.*
Early pioneers when Ste-Agathe was the northern frontier.

Harris, R. Cole and Warrentin, John. *Canada Before Confederation.*
Oxford University Press, Toronto, 1974.

Johannsen, Alice E. *The Legendary Jackrabbit Johannsen.*
McGill-Queen's University Press, Montreal, 1993.
A full scale well written biography of the "Chief".

Lamarche, Jacques. *Au Coeur de la Petite-Nation. Le Château Montebello.*
Les Éditions de la Petite-Nation, Ottawa, 1984.

Laurin, Serge. *Histoire des Laurentides.*
Diffusion Prologue Inc., Saint-Laurent, Québec, 1989.
Authoritative and comprehensive information on the Laurentian region.

Lewis, Jefferson. *Something Hidden. A Biography of Wilder Penfield.*
Doubleday, Ltd., Toronto, 1981.
An informative biography of a renowned Canadian doctor.

Lund, Rolf Tonning. *A History of Skiing in Canada Prior to 1940.*
Unpublished M.A. Thesis. University of Alberta, Edmonton, 1971.
Contains a cornucopia of little known material.

Mitchell, George D. *Heritage Daldurn.*
A good account of the Durnfords and other Laurentian pioneers.

O'Rear, John and Frankie. *The Mont Tremblant Story.*
Les Éditions Altitude, Mont-Tremblant, 1988.
Informative text with many excellent photographs.

Paré, Lucy Griffith. *The Seeds: The Life Story of a Matriarch.*
Les Entreprises de l'Arpent Perdu Inc. Ste-Lucie-des Laurentides, Québec
Splendid memoir of an interesting woman and her memories of Montreal and the Laurentians.

Wilder Penfield, M.D. *No Man Alone.*
Little, Brown and Company, Boston, 1977.
Engaging personal account of his early years in Montreal.

Powell, Brian, ed. *Jackrabbit: His First Hundred Years.*
Collier Macmillan, Toronto, 1975.
Colourful recollections of the "Chief" by those who knew him.

Rumilly, Robert. *Histoire de Montréal, Tome 3.*
Fides, Montréal, 1972.

Stewart, Anita (with George Wieser). *The Gray Rocks Story.*
Wieser & Wieser, New York, 1988.
Colourful written and pictorial story of the Wheelers.

Turner Bone, Allan. *Souvenir of 50 Years in the Life of the Laurentian Lodge Club Inc.*, 1973.
Delightful account of the early years by someone who was there for most of them.

Wheeler, Frances. *The Awakening of the Laurentians.*
Vintage Press, New York, 1959.
Personal memories of the beginning of Gray Rocks.

Credit of uncaptioned illustrations in the last chapter, "A Magical Place":

Painting by Elena Larkin, CPR Collection, Drawing donated by Arthur Terroux, L.L.C. Collection, CPR Collection.

Charter Members

William Gordon Hanson
Hugh A. Johnston
Grant Johnston
Leslie Frederick Skelton
John Henry Van Sickels
J. A. Cameron
T. C. Cook
Don Cleghorn
W. H. Knowles
C. W. Kennedy
G.H.E. Molson
W. E. Macfarlane
C. B. Pitblado
J. Ross Robertson
H. G. Welsford

Presidents

1924-29	N. M. Yuile
1930	Walter Merrill
1931	John McEntyre
1932	Chas McNicol
1933-35	Kirk McLeod
1936	Brock Thomson
1937	Lindsay Hall
1938	A. S. Rutherford
1939	Gen. E. Panet
1940	Gordon Hanson
1941-43	E. A. Millar
1944	W. S. Yuile
1945	G. A. Birks
1946	Cy Kennedy
1947	C. K. Trim
1948	J. C. Cushing
1949	H. C. Harragin
1950	H. K. McLean
1951	W. Sutherland
1952	W. F. Pratt
1953	A. Turner Bone
1954	A. L. Williams
1955	D. A. Baillie
1956	P. B. Reid
1957	A. Ross Webster
1958-59	J. S. Hewson
1960	W. A. Eversfield
1961-62	J. T. Thompson
1963	T. Denton Lewis
1964	Binnie Fairbanks
1965	A. M. Weldon
1966	H. F. Stanfield
1967	A. H. Capper
1968	D. C. Hannaford
1969	P. B. Reid
1970	Ken Farmer
1971	Paul Dawson/Henry Yates
1972	Walter Hotson
1973	Michael Tucker
1974	John Stephenson
1975	Eman Newcomb
1976	Frank Nemec
1977	Bev Baily
1978	Duncan Howard
1979	Duncan Howard
1980	Rick Sargent
1981	Rick Sargent
1982	Albert Nixon
1983	Albert Nixon
1984	Norma Rollit
1985	Norma Rollit
1986	Bob Gibb
1987	Scott Taylor
1988	Scott Taylor
1989	Ian Mair
1990	Ian Mair
1991	Norm Chinn
1992	Norm Chinn
1993	Dick Tremaine
1994	Dick Tremaine
1995	Rudiger Pahl
1996	Rudiger Pahl
1997	Jim Moore
1998	Jim Moore
1999	Barrie Wilson
2000	Barrie Wilson

Contributors of stories to this book

Allan Aitken
Ginnie (Birks) Alexandor
Eleanor Algie
Gerry Allen
Natalie (Harding) Anderson
Peggy (Johannsen) Austin
Bev Baily
Betty (Meek) Beeby
Janice (Perry) Bernabucci
Norman Blachford
Ann (Jarvis) Boa
Jeannette Brooker
Mabel (Selby) Bryson
May Buick
Andrea (Rutherford) Burgess
Isabel (McGill) Cameron
Nan Carlin
Taylor Carlin
Priscilla (Penfield) Chester
Betty (Buchanan) Chinn
Joan (Ross) Clark
Joan Cleather
Louis Cochand
Susan Craig
George Currie
Cleveland Dodge
Phyllis Dodge
William Doyle
Denis Drummond
Michael Drummond
Sally (Sharwood) Drummond
Jean (Peters) Dupont
Sue (Birks) Dwyer
Elizabeth (Angus) Eberts
John Elder
Ken Farmer
Bill and Faith Feindel
Joan (Radley) Fitzpatrick
Karen Foster
Zib Fraser
John Fry
Larry Garmaise
Sheila (Wallis) Gilbert
Kenneth Hague
Nancy (Birks) Hale
Frances (McLeod) Hamilton
Carol (Reaper) Harrison
Michael Hayes
Ned Heney
John Henry
Bob Hill
Orian (Stewart) Hodgson
Eric Hotson
Andrew K. Hugessen
Jim Hugessen
Chris Hyde
Marigold (Savage) Hyde
Judy Jaques
Eleanor (Lindsay) Jarrett
Barbara Kemp
Haagen Kierulf
Bruce Kippen
Walter Lee
Geoffrey Lehman
Libby (Wallace) Leslie
Herbie Lewis
Jane (Yuile) Lewis
Susan Lincoln
Nancy (Durnford) Lorimer
Elizabeth (Turner Bone) and Douglas MacEwan
Bev MacInnes
Betty Maxwell
Virginia (Welsford) McClure
Joan (McMaster) McKim
Lois (Ibbotson) McTaggart
Charlotte Millen
Mary Anne (Currie) Miller
Ellen and Jim Moore
Tim Morris
Anne (Henry) Murdoch
Philippa Newcomb
Albert Nixon
Laurie O'Brien
Phil O'Brien
Karin (Austin) O'Gorman
Lynn (Rutherford) O'Reilly
Jill Pangman
Susan and Rudiger Pahl
Senator Landon Mackenzie Pearson
André Pelrine
Jeff Penfield
Charles Peters
Pat Pettigrew
John Pitblado
Mary Jane (Miles) Ramsay
Banty Reid
F. A. Reid
Bart Reilly
Ann and David Robinson
Jackie (Beaudoin) Ross
Joan and Mel Rothman
Bruce and Jane Russel
Bob Sargent
Heather Sargent
John Schwab
Gary Selby
Hugh Seybold
Gordon Shaw
Margaret Shirriff
Linda (Thompson) Sinclair
Beverly (Mellen) Sofin
Louise Spalding
William Stavert
Vincent Thorburn
Diana (Drew) Togneri
George Trim
John Trim
Michael Tucker
John Turner Bone
Hugh Wallis
Mary (Fry) Wang
Garnice Ware
Margaret (Turner Bone) Watt
Boyd Whittall
Helen (Tucker) Wiegand
Adela (Bartholomew)Wilmerding
Barbara Winn
Jeff, Frances and Russ Williams
Barry and Elizabeth Wilson
Anne (Hale) Wonham
Henry Yates

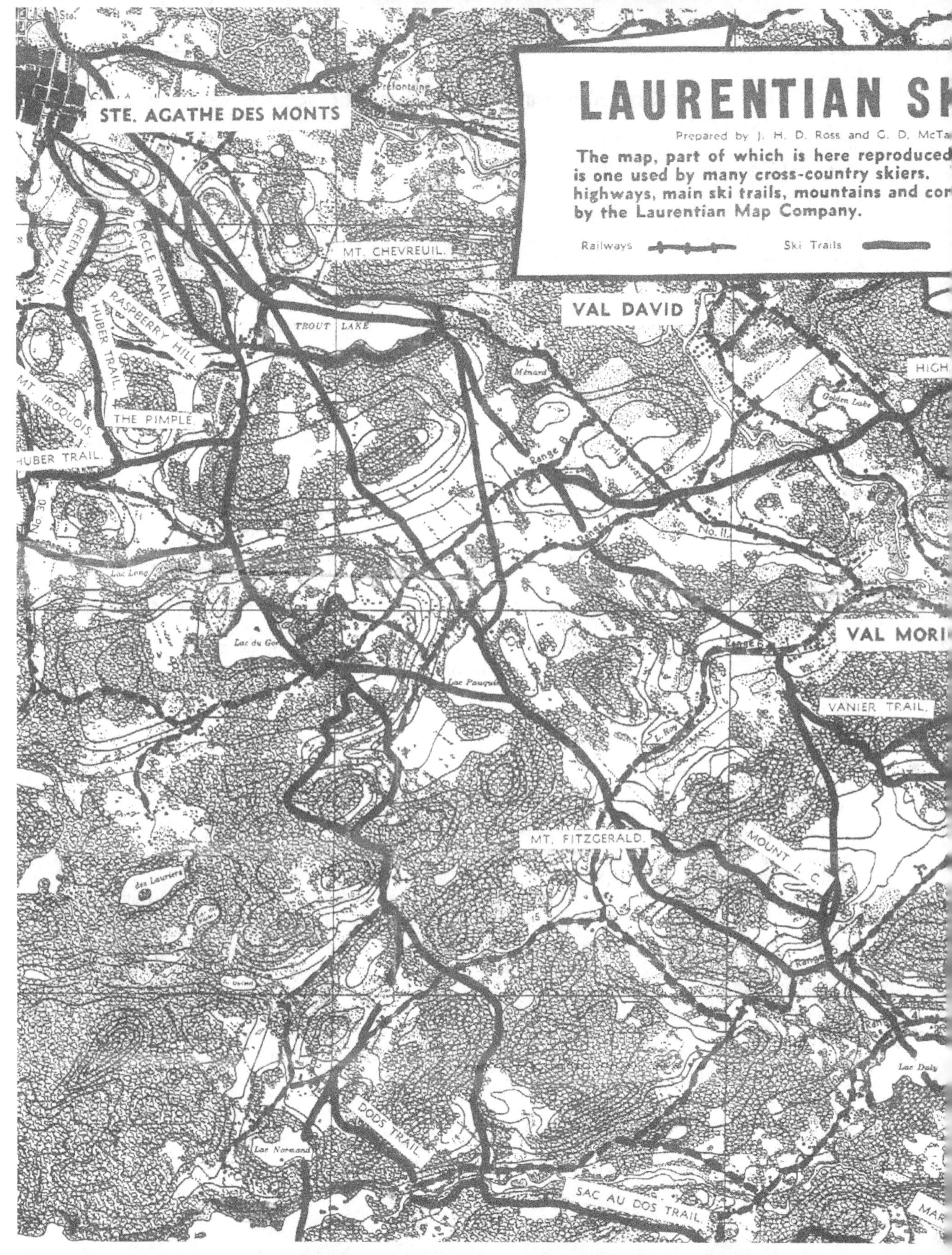
LAURENTIAN SK
Prepared by J. H. D. Ross and C. D. McTa
The map, part of which is here reproduced
is one used by many cross-country skiers.
highways, main ski trails, mountains and co
by the Laurentian Map Company.
Railways
Ski Trails
STE. AGATHE DES MONTS
Préfontaine
MT. CHEVREUIL.
GREEN HILL
CIRCLE TRAIL.
RASPBERRY HILL
HUBER TRAIL.
MT. IROQUOIS.
THE PIMPLE.
HUBER TRAIL.
TROUT LAKE
VAL DAVID
L. Ménard
Golden Lake
HIGH
Range 8
Highway
Range 7
No. 11.
No. 30
Lac Long
Lac du Go
Lac Pasqui
VAL MORI
VANIER TRAIL.
L. Roy
MT. FITZGERALD.
MOUNT I. C.
des Lauriers
Lac Daly
DODS TRAIL.
Lac Normand
SAC AU DOS TRAIL.
MAR

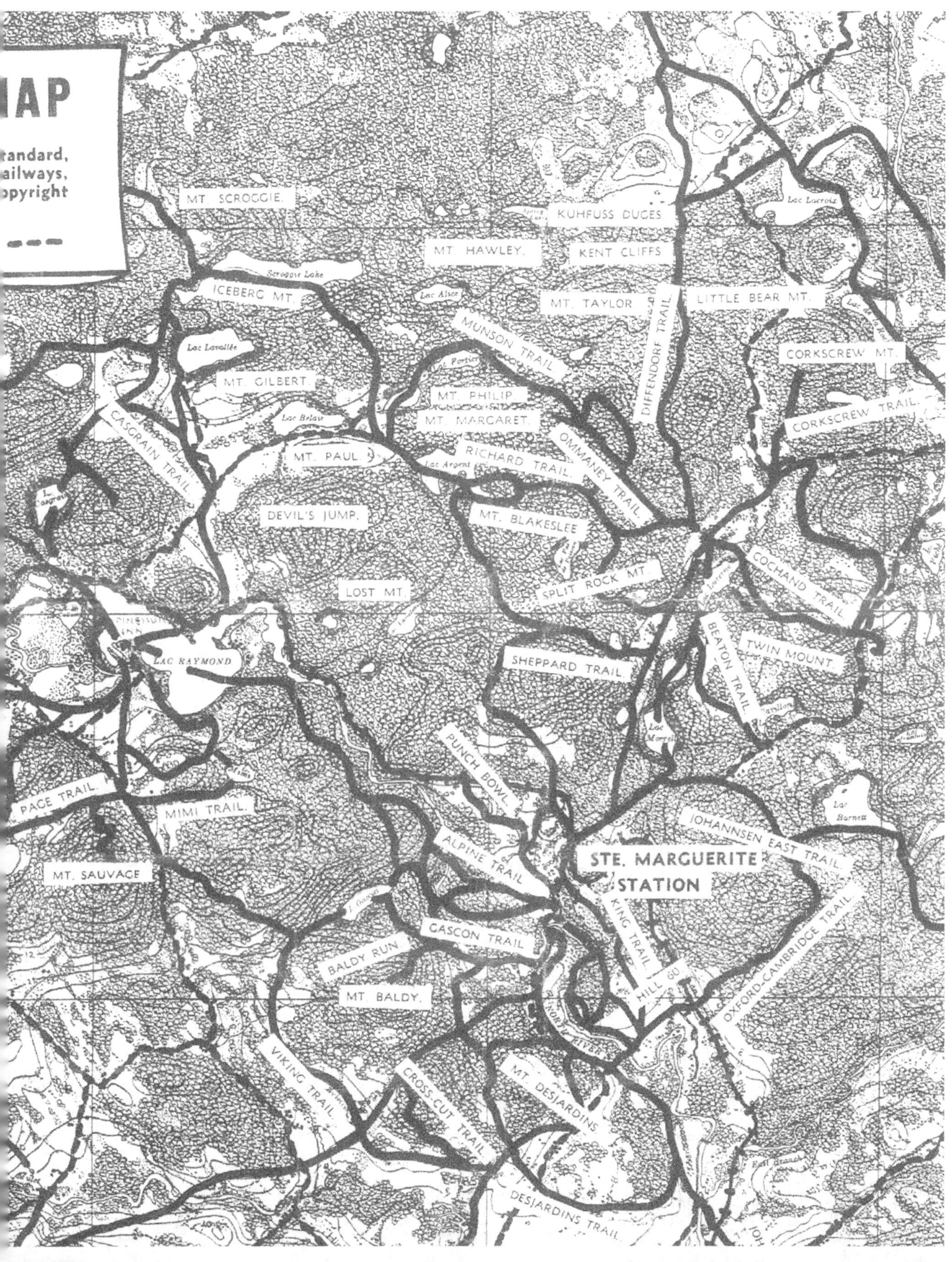
MT. SCROGGIE.
Scroggie Lake
KUHFUSS DUCES.
MT. HAWLEY.
KENT CLIFFS
Lac Lacroix
ICEBERG MT.
Lac Alice
MT. TAYLOR
DIFFENDORF TRAIL
LITTLE BEAR MT.
Lac Lavallée
MUNSON TRAIL
CORKSCREW MT.
MT. GILBERT.
MT. PHILIP.
MT. MARGARET.
CORKSCREW TRAIL.
CASGRAIN TRAIL
Lac Belair
MT. PAUL.
RICHARD TRAIL.
Lac Argent
OMMANEY TRAIL
DEVIL'S JUMP.
MT. BLAKESLEE
SPLIT ROCK MT.
COCHAND TRAIL
LOST MT.
LAC RAYMOND
SHEPPARD TRAIL.
BEATON TRAIL
TWIN MOUNT.
PUNCH BOWL
PAGE TRAIL.
MIMI TRAIL.
Lac Barnett
JOHANNSEN EAST TRAIL.
ALPINE TRAIL
MT. SAUVAGE
STE. MARGUERITE
STATION
KING TRAIL
GASCON TRAIL
BALDY RUN.
OXFORD-CAMBRIDGE TRAIL
HILL 60
MT. BALDY.
NORTH RIVER
VIKING TRAIL
CROSS-CUT TRAIL
MT. DESJARDINS
DESJARDINS TRAIL

www.ingramcontent.com/pod-product-compliance
Lightning Source LLC
LaVergne TN
LVHW081300100826
845148LV00005B/933
* 9 7 8 1 6 1 1 5 3 0 8 3 4 *